"While all of us as leaders of growing organizations seem to know what makes us successful, Lewis and McKone do an uncanny job of pushing the reader to ask the tough question of what more can be done to unlock the potential to drive market share and margin growth. *Edge Strategy* 'takes the blinders off' and helps you look around corners for opportunities that may be missed in strategic planning sessions."

   —GEOFF BALLOTTI, President and CEO, Wyndham Hotel Group

"M&A and new business development may garner newspaper headlines, but Lewis and McKone guide the reader in identifying and capturing growth with less risk. This book urges greater attention on foundational business assets and customers. It deserves a thoughtful read and extended discussion."

   —BRIAN BETHERS, CEO and Chairman, 1-800 CONTACTS

"In this compelling book, Alan Lewis and Dan McKone show how to take on an 'edge strategy' mindset, enabling you to continually identify and unlock the great value that exists at the edge of your business. A great read!"

   —MICHAEL E. FOSS, CEO, Sports Authority

"*Edge Strategy* will inspire you to think about growth opportunities in a new and powerful way. Through insightful examples and a well-structured process, the concepts presented in the book provide a framework for identifying the opportunities that lie at the doorstep of many businesses ready to be leveraged by the organization's various assets with limited risk and significant upside."

   —ARI N. HASEOTES, CEO, The Cumberland Gulf Group

"The approach put forward in *Edge Strategy* has helped us effectively frame and evaluate our growth opportunities. It provides a road map that considers internal capabilities, customer behavior and preferences, and the elements of differentiation."

   —JULIET JOHANSSON, Executive Vice President and Chief Strategy Officer, Office Depot, Inc.

"For any executive or manager who wants a practical, realistic guide to increasing growth in their business, look no further. Lewis and McKone do a remarkable job of making the journey both informative and enjoyable."

   —HARRY M. JANSEN KRAEMER JR., Professor, Northwestern University's Kellogg School of Management; former Chairman and CEO, Baxter International; and author, *From Values to Action* and *Becoming the Best*

"We've learned that the most effective way to extract profits from our business is to focus on the core. But that leaves a big question unanswered: How do you grow? Lewis and McKone offer clear insight on how to grow the enterprise using edge strategy. A must-read."

—JIM LAWRENCE, former CFO, Unilever and General Mills

"*Edge Strategy* is a must-read for any executive trying to chart successful and profitable growth. Lewis and McKone elegantly outline a clear path toward focusing on the low-hanging fruits that will surely lead to great results for any business."

—PATRICK SALYER, CEO, Gigya

"Successful companies continually look to emerging markets or underserved areas in the core business where assets, competencies, and culture can be leveraged. Alan Lewis and Dan McKone's *Edge Strategy* provides valuable insights into this journey. It provides a road map for identifying and understanding opportunities often considered 'at the margin' of the core business, and then deploying core assets and services in a different yet complementary way to unlock new value for customers— and generate new revenues for the core business. It's a thought-provoking narrative for any executive."

—DOUGLAS W. STOTLAR, President and CEO, Con-way Inc.

"Strategy doesn't have to be about big shifts or leaps. It's often about taking the competitive advantages you already have and figuring out how to expand or apply them to new products, markets, or business lines. In this insightful yet deeply practical book, Lewis and McKone provide an indispensable guide to tackling this challenge."

—KATHLEEN TAYLOR, former President and CEO, Four Seasons Hotels & Resorts

"With *Edge Strategy*, Alan Lewis and Dan McKone have given us, regardless of whether our endeavors are for-profit or not, a cogent and impactful reminder of how important it is to think beyond historical or traditional boundaries and to imagine a result that we have not yet experienced . . . and then go for it. As they clearly demonstrate with their examples of edge strategy, the results can be the difference between revitalization and failure."

—GLENN TILTON, former CEO and Chairman, United Airlines and Texaco Inc.

EDGE
STRATEGY

EDGE
STRATEGY

A New
Mindset *for*
Profitable
Growth

HARVARD BUSINESS
REVIEW PRESS
Boston, Massachusetts

ALAN LEWIS
DAN MCKONE

The web addresses referenced in this book were live and correct at the time of the book's publication but may be subject to change.

Library of Congress Cataloging-in-Publication Data

Lewis, Alan, 1975- author. McKone, Dan, author.
  Edge strategy: a new mindset for profitable growth / Alan Lewis and Dan McKone.
  Boston, Massachusetts: Harvard Business Review Press, [2015]
  Includes bibliographical references and index.
  LCCN 2015033353
  ISBN 9781633690172 (alk. paper)
  Strategic planning. Marketing. Management.

LCC HD30.28 .L4936 2015 DDC 658.4/012—dc23 LC record available at http://lccn.loc.gov/2015033353

CONTENTS

Preface: An Alternative Path to Growth   *vii*

PART ONE

The Edge Framework and Mindset

Chapter 1   THE EDGE EFFECT: 3
              Why Edges Are Powerful

Chapter 2   EDGE OF THE PRODUCT: 21
              Rescoping the Boundaries of Your Offer

Chapter 3   EDGE OF THE JOURNEY: 33
              Completing the Customer's Mission

Chapter 4   EDGE OF THE ENTERPRISE: 49
              Viewing Your Assets from the Outside

PART TWO

Where to Unlock Value

Chapter 5   EFFECTIVE UPSELLING: 65
              Redefining "Even Better" Solutions

Chapter 6   DEALING WITH MARGIN PRESSURE: 87
              Staying Profitable Despite Headwinds

Chapter 7   BEATING THE COMMODITIZATION CYCLE: 105
             Sharpening Differentiation with Less Risk

Chapter 8   THE EDGE OF BIG DATA: 121
             Enabling New Ways to Create Value

Chapter 9   A NEW MINDSET FOR M&A: 137
             Getting Real Value from Synergies

Chapter 10   FINDING YOUR EDGE: 161
             A Ten-Step Guide

Notes   183
Index   199
Acknowledgments   209
About the Authors   211

PREFACE

An Alternative Path to Growth

During many years analyzing and advising hundreds of companies, we have observed a simple but distinct pattern in the fabric of corporate strategy. Our research demonstrates that this recurring theme exists in all sixty-two industries in the Standard & Poor's (S&P) index. We have witnessed this phenomenon in large companies and small, worldwide, and over time. The familiar aspect of the pattern is that the best prospects for driving profits tend to leverage resources and capabilities that your organization already knows. The less intuitive aspect is that the best leverage often exists at the "edge" of your business model.

Our business focuses on improving other businesses. As a result, we see companies striving, reaching, and bending, quite literally contorting their business models in search of a way to augment their bottom lines. However, we have found that many of these companies struggle to advance with the traditional growth strategies.

The issue for most firms, regardless of industry, is that they seem to be programmed to simply do *more* of what they do best: extending their presence to more regions, expanding their range to more customers, or just plain selling more stuff. We often find that companies are so focused on doing more of what they do every day that they start to think everything in their organization has a singular purpose. They understand the purchase process inside out, they drive vendors and channels, and they chart operational flows in NASA-worthy detail, all in ruthless pursuit of optimization.

The problem with "more" is that it only works for a while. There are only so many locations, so many customers, and so much output that is in demand until saturation occurs. Even when companies think that they have plenty of rows to till in their particular fields, they turn around to find familiar or new competitors, squatting on their land and harvesting their crops. The inevitable market-share game also proves a fool's errand, a war of attrition where even the cleverest of core strategies is ultimately copied, resulting in a return to a similar equilibrium.

Companies are eventually motivated to look for growth in far-flung places. Typically, this means acquiring rival companies; developing adjacent, but quite different, businesses; or searching for "blue oceans" of uncontested market space. The trouble with these strategies is that while the rewards can be high, so too can the odds of failure.

The myopia associated with core business perfectionism often blinds us to the value of what we already have. Looking around for new bets, companies also tend to overlook a significant, untapped source of profit that exists in the near field—on the edge of the core business, through the sale of ancillary goods and services that actually make existing customers' interaction with the business more complete.

We call this "edge strategy." Unlike many accepted approaches, edge strategy focuses on gains that are easily within a company's grasp. It shines a new light on the latent leverage that companies already have, and as a result, it requires less up-front investment and less risk.

Edge Strategy:
An Alternative Path to Growth

Often, the periphery of your core business, rather than the core itself or some distant horizon, is richest with opportunity. We have identified scores of organizations that have unlocked value by exploring what we call their "edges" and, by doing so, get more yield from assets already in place, access already established, and investments already made. When an organization relaxes its assumptions of what exactly it does, what exactly its customers want from it (or who else might have a different use for what it has acquired or built along the way), the result can be profound. Developing this insight is the essence of edge strategy.

Edge opportunities are available to more companies precisely because they are modest by definition. They also provide a sensible path to innovation in that they build on what is already resident. Some attractive, but frequently observed characteristics of edge strategies include:

- Profit margins that are often greater than those generated by the core business.

- Risk, and up-front investment, that is lower, given leverage from existing assets.

- Power to address a greater number of fragmented customer needs, increasing the overall value proposition for each customer.

- Upside that is incremental, not only to the company but also the market; that is, edge revenue doesn't necessarily have to be captured from competitors.

- Significant improvement in customer satisfaction via better calibration to customer needs.

Our goal with this book is to instill in you the ability to recognize and take advantage of edge strategies: what we call an *edge mindset*. To do this, we provide a practical and visual framework that characterizes three different kinds of edge strategy. We provide a wide range of examples across industries and geographies that illustrates how companies have employed these strategies and how they have benefited. We consider familiar situations that your business may be experiencing to set the context for where each kind of edge strategy could have the most impact for you. We provide a ten-step process for how you can find and gain leverage from edge opportunities in your company.

Empowered with an edge mindset, any executive or manager in any company, large or small, in any industry, has the ability to find and realize new sources of profitable growth.

PART
ONE

THE EDGE
FRAMEWORK
AND MINDSET

CHAPTER 1

THE EDGE EFFECT

Why Edges Are Powerful

Everyone is looking for an edge, or advantage, in business. How do we win? How do we get ahead? What is the angle that will drive our company's success? But an edge is not just a term for advantage itself; it can also be the place where you can *find* that advantage.

We define an "edge" as the outer rim that frames what you do and separates it, quite conveniently, from what you don't. Edges are frontiers beyond which something changes. When you proceed beyond this border in business, the main thing that changes is risk (see figure 1-1).

Edges are not necessarily clear. To the contrary, many edges are quite fuzzy. When you look to the horizon, are you always sure where the sea ends and the sky begins? In business, strategy edges are like that too. Rare is the exact definition of how a product is positioned, what value a product delivers, or where different customers give a business permission to play. We argue that opportunity resides in this very ambiguity. If its edges are not well defined, a business can redefine them, ever so slightly, in its favor. And by staying within this nebulous but familiar space instead of moving to the less comfortable adjacent expanse or

FIGURE 1-1

The outer rim or "edge" of your business

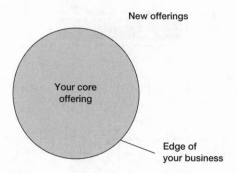

The edge of your business is the delineation of where your current offering begins and ends.

beyond, a business can find brilliant new ways to leverage its existing assets.

Edges have another interesting property; they are the places where the inside and the outside meet. As such, they tend to be where the action is. In nature, in civilization, and, indeed, in business, the peripheries teem with the most fascinating interactions. Where things meet, opportunities abound. Let's start there.

The Edge Effect

Ecologists call the phenomenon we just described "the edge effect." In the 1930s, Aldo Leopold, an American environmentalist, coined the term when explaining why quail, grouse, and other game birds were more prevalent in transitional agricultural landscapes than in single (homogenous) habitats like fields and forests. He posited that "the desirability of simultaneous access to more than one habitat" and "the greater richness of edge vegetation" supported a greater diversity and abundance of species.[1]

Since then, scientists have given these borderlands a name—"ecotones." Eugene Odum, whose classic text, *Fundamentals of Ecology*, helped to popularize this idea in the 1950s, described an ecotone as "an area or zone of transition between two or more diverse communities."[2] He was thinking about the border between forest and grassland or between sea and shore. Places of transition between two ecosystems, such as the edge of forests, shorelines, wetlands, cliffs and mountain sides, estuaries, savannah, tundra, and deserts, are where the greatest diversity and opportunity exist for both flora and fauna. At the edges, the populations, resources, nutrients, lights, and food from both ecosystems mix. Some species exist *only* in ecotones, given the uniquely fertile environment that the combination of the two worlds creates.[3]

Odum's work illuminated why these transitions are particularly fecund and helped explain why 90 percent of marine species live within the 10 percent of ocean nearest the shore.[4] But the edge effect also helps to answer other questions that stretch far beyond the natural world.

For instance, why is it that 75 percent of Canadians live within a hundred miles of the US border?[5] Here, along a 4,400-mile stretch of land, lies the possibility of doing business with the biggest economy in the world.[6] Throughout history, people have focused on edges and built ports—literally, "doors" or gateways—to facilitate trade between different communities that exist on either side.

Karl Polanyi, a Hungarian-American economist, has written extensively on the subject of "ports of trade," providing detailed explanation of how these locations served to drive the cogs of the economy and commerce from as long ago as 2000 BC.[7] These edges are highly varied. Terrel Gallaway, expanding on the work of Polanyi, noted that "[p]orts of trade, like any ecotone, cannot be defined in solely spatial terms."[8] These crossroads also promote the establishment of the enablers of commerce. Some, such as Hong Kong or Singapore, are located on the coast. Others, such as Timbuktu, an old Saharan caravan town linking ancient trade routes, are located on the edge of the desert. Istanbul was built on a border where continents meet—the blurred area that is neither exactly Europe nor Asia, but has a strong cultural influence from both.

It is no surprise that academics draw parallels between the ecotones of nature and the "economic ecotones" of ports of trade and even extend the logic further to the routes that exist between them. Typically, these are also situated at the edges between civilizations. Great trade routes have seeded the major cities of the world and been the conduits for advancement. "Such a river of life as nowhere else exists in the world" is how Rudyard Kipling described the collection of cultural meeting points that make up the Grand Trunk Road.[9]

Three Types of Business Ecotones

We can also apply this concept of ecotones to individual businesses, to powerful effect. In our work, we have observed that this "transitional bonanza," this "opportunity between things," is alive and well at the level of individual corporations. As in nature, these phenomena are often familiar; once recognized, they may even seem obvious. However, before they are exploited, they must be spotted. Consider the many edges that frame a business.

First, there is the boundary where you and your customers come together. Of all the activities that an organization undertakes, this transition is the most important and certainly where all the money is generated. But just like the ecotones we discussed, the lines around a product or service are often imprecise (see figure 1-2). Companies frequently misgauge the desires of their customers, and those customers, in turn, can misconstrue the propositions of companies.

If you have ever been to a theme park or taken a cruise, you will recognize what we mean. While you could consider the booking or ticket of admission as your payment to enjoy all these suppliers have to offer—and, indeed, you have no obligation to spend any more to participate—you know that you are presented with endless opportunities to enhance your experience for a small (or not so small) incremental charge. These companies are masters of navigating the blurred lines around their core product.

Second, the temporal component of this interaction creates its own edges. In our nature analogy, the disruption and coming together,

FIGURE 1-2

Opportunities at the edge

New offerings

Your core
offering

Opportunity
at the edge of
your business

The edge of your business is rarely a sharp perimeter but rather a nexus of opportunity.

which occurs at the twilight transition between day and night, presents unique opportunities for animals to feed. As a result, a host of mammals, birds, and insects are most active during these times.[10] Businesses, too, focus on temporal transitions. The relationship with customers can span everything from an exploratory shopping event to a lifetime of commerce. Even slightly modifying this period of interaction—the edge where the customer relationship begins and ends—is intuitively powerful.

Consider your own search for food. We expect that if you were in a grocery store today, you wouldn't have given a second thought to the opportunities such a business has with a product as mundane as lettuce. Yet, someone had the insight to see that the journey to a meal for a customer who buys a head of lettuce isn't complete: he has to wash it and chop it first before consuming it. This simple insight enabled the transformation of a commodity produce item to a highly profitable prepared food. As we will explore in chapter 3, helping the consumer by going a step further is now an important way that companies like Whole Foods Market have transformed their economics and enhanced their relationship with the customer.

Third, there are all the assets, tangible and intangible, that collectively define a business. These have edges, too. If an enterprise takes careful inventory, it will find that many of the parameters that describe what is core and noncore to its business are equally vague. It may even find that there is some room for interpretation in the very use of these resources and capabilities. In this way, the edges of assets themselves create opportunities.

You may not be surprised that a company like Toyota uses technology it installs in all the cars it sells in Japan to produce data that powers its onboard GPS service. You may be more interested to know that Toyota recognized that the value of this data was not uniquely associated with its primary use. As we will discover in chapter 8, this insight enabled Toyota to successfully launch a new business offering traffic telematics services to businesses and municipalities across Japan using the same data.

Companies Are Stacks of Foundational Assets

Most corporate mission statements and strategies attempt to answer some variation of the question, "What are we best at?" Firms tend to answer this question—and base their entire identities—by referring to their foundational assets. These can take the form of hard assets, such as a fleet of airplanes or a chain of retail stores. Or they can take the form of more intangible assets, such as smart employees or strong intellectual property based on a given skill.

Every business has a stack of foundational assets that contributes to the delivery of its core offering. At the bottom of this stack are any hard resources that your firm might have: land, buildings, equipment, mining rights, what have you. Above these are typically some softer resources: your labor force, the data you collect, and so on. On top of these lie the capabilities that you employ, the particular skills your company has acquired and honed over the years to make it more effective in its core business. At the top of the stack lies the more metaphysical

FIGURE 1-3

A company's foundational assets

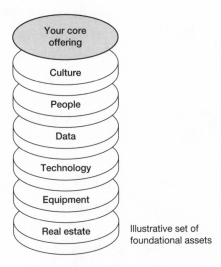

Illustrative set of foundational assets

Your enterprise is built on a unique set of foundational assets to deliver your core offering.

properties of your organization—the culture, the ethos, the stuff that makes your company unique (see figure 1-3).

These foundational assets are important. They help form the barriers to entry a company fosters to protect its market share. In most cases, these assets are the basis of how companies compete and seek to differentiate themselves from rival companies; they are the tools of the (win-lose) competition at the core of most corporate strategies today.

Players who invest early and well—or perhaps are a bit lucky—can capture a dominant position in their market that then creates the platform to sustain this advantage, returning the cost of capital and keeping shareholders happy. These are the core strategy winners, the exceptional performers. The first problem is that few (if any) companies are able to sustain core dominance over the long term. The second, bigger problem is that by definition, this route to success doesn't even apply to most companies.

Rarely do most (if not all) companies realize the inherent value of their foundational assets. Despite their complexity, foundational assets are typically built to execute on a relatively narrow set of activities, delivering the core offering of the company and, ideally, doing so better than competitors. Companies typically devote much less time to additional, creative ways that they can leverage these assets.

Deriving Leverage from Foundational Assets

In our edge analogies, fundamental systems have evolved that allow magic to happen at the places of transition. Life is abundant at the ocean edge because a confluence of interactions there makes gathering nourishment easier.[11] The twilight migration creates similar conditions for predators; the relative effort of hunting at a nexus of activity is a fraction of what is required to stalk the forest at a more sedentary hour.[12] Converging on a hub like Singapore is a decidedly easier way to trade than to travel to each individual spoke of a merchant network. In all of these edge examples, the common theme is that the system that supports the transition space creates leverage.

In business applications, edge opportunities are precisely focused on gaining this additional leverage. Assembling the original machinery, network, or relationship that makes meaningful results possible requires considerable effort. But once the infrastructure is built, the marginal return from greater utilization is exceptionally high. We will keep returning to this fundamental principle: there is great power in tapping latent potential. When a company identifies these opportunities, unlocking them requires only the incremental cost of modifying an existing system of foundational assets. By contrast, the cost for a new entrant to assemble these same assets from scratch is considerable.

We described three types of business ecotones or situations where edges can occur—in the definition of a product, the nature of the customer relationship, and the use of assets themselves. Each of these interaction spaces is made possible by the foundational assets a company has deployed to execute on its core strategy. The question comes down to where this system of assets can be equipped with more flexibility. Where can these foundational assets be toggled to create options— options that can help you differentiate customers and capture much more than you could with an average solution?

As we'll see later in this book, companies in industries as diverse as telecom, retail, cruise lines, and medical devices have all created these options. In so doing, they have accessed incremental revenue streams carrying profit margins that are many times what their core businesses realized. This is not magic. It is clever piggybacking on what has largely already been built.

Why Edges Are Less Risky

One of our principle claims is that edge strategies are inherently less risky than many other alternatives a business has to grow revenue and profit. At the surface, this may appear fundamentally at odds with the higher-return characteristics we have outlined.

Part of the reason edges can be simultaneously higher return and lower risk is that the risk is paid for elsewhere. When foundational assets are deployed, in support of the core business, they need to pass their own return-on-investment standard. The investment to establish and preserve foundational assets is typically predicated completely on core performance. Unless a company explicitly contemplated an edge opportunity as an option in the original business model, its discovery is a bit of boon. It requires *some incremental effort*, through investment or configuration, but more or less benefits from the system of assets that supports the core. In this way, edge opportunities are additional dividends from your core business.

Another reason is that most growth alternatives tend to be new ventures that involve significant uncertainty in the translation of a business case into reality and unforeseen complexities and costs that might arise.

It could relate to less predictable market forces, because "new venture" implies that a company has less experience upon which it can rely. Or, quite simply, it could be the greater unknown of how customers will react to a new proposition, a new product form factor, or a new way of engaging through the channel of choice.

Edge strategies face similar uncertainties; the difference is in the degree. First, because edge strategies are aimed at harvesting more value from existing assets, enabling them tends to require a relatively lower level of capital outlay, that is, less new money at risk. This is not to say that they require no investment, but merely that the risk profile is very different from, say, a venture starting without the benefit of the same foundational assets. Second, edge strategy is, by definition, a calibration story. It does not involve stepping out into a new space that is not well understood. It is about reframing or repurposing very familiar interactions in a way that releases pent-up demand.

As such, the endgame of edge strategy is often not transformational, but it is readily realizable in a way that does not compromise the objectives of the core business. As such, edge strategy tends to be an approach that pragmatists favor.

Asking the Right Questions

The goal is to discover new and lucrative ways to monetize your company's foundational assets. The approach is to look beyond the core business to near-field offerings, where the most leverage (and, intriguingly, the least risk) resides. As with many worthwhile endeavors, the challenge is in knowing where to start.

Frequently, companies focusing on their core business ask themselves: "What are we best at?" This is an important question, of course. But the danger is that it can make the company too introspective, too distracted by its own competencies, and not sufficiently focused on the customer.

To find an edge opportunity, we propose starting with a different set of questions:

- What do our different types of customers want (or need)?

- What could or should our solution include?

- Which of our assets would others value and why?

This framework is competencies-based (inward out) rather than needs-based (outward in), and much more naturally centers on the customer—the absolute key to any profit-expansion effort. It is the best vantage point from which to begin a search. When you review a business this way, in the context of the three types of business ecotones discussed earlier, you orient the process to identify three corresponding types of opportunities. We call these product edges, journey edges, and enterprise edges.

The first, *product edges*, are the most prevalent. They arise when a product or service is imperfectly calibrated with some customers' needs. With product edges, an opportunity exists to provide either more or less to certain customer segments in order to better satisfy their overall requirements. Some examples of this might be add-on accessories, complementary services, or options to extend, enhance, or modify a base offer. Each of these strategies creates a better configuration of the core offer for the needs of each unique customer.

The second, *journey edges*, recast the nature of a company's relationship with the customer in a way that better maps to the customer's ultimate objective. We think of customers as being on "journeys"—or missions to do or accomplish something. From this, it follows that any product or service is merely a step along the way to achieving a bigger goal. Journey edges refer to opportunities in which companies redefine their participation in the customer's journey and expand their solution to encompass needs that either immediately precede or follow the core transaction. For example, when someone buys a flat-screen TV, he has to get it out of the box, assemble it, install it, and program it. In other words, the customer's journey does not end when he walks away from the cash register with his new TV. Accordingly, options that wrap service around product, anything that turns "do it yourself" into "do it for me," is a journey edge.

The third, *enterprise edges*, are the most challenging to find. They are not necessarily intuitive, and an introspective focus on the core can actually hamper the lateral thinking required to identify them. The idea with enterprise edges is to exploit foundational assets in ways that were not foreseen when they were developed to support the core business. Somewhere in the stack of these assets, inadvertent value could be buried. Like other edges, the asset already exists, and under the right conditions, almost accidently, it might enable most of what is necessary to satisfy an unintended need elsewhere. As we will see later in the book, data is an intuitive example. Companies often collect rich data in the process of running their core operation that also happens to be valuable to other companies. As a consequence, it often takes only incremental investment to monetize this value by applying the data in another context.

The Space Between

You may be wondering how this strategic framework fits with others you are familiar with. Simply put, it is complementary. Just as edge opportunities exist somewhere in between your product and what is beyond it, so too should you view the role of edge strategy relative to core strategy and strategies for building new ventures.

You likely employ a range of strategic tools and techniques to expand your market share or to develop new products to pit against your competition. You may also explore opportunities to improve your position on your value chain, better orchestrate suppliers and customers, or gain better access to profit pools. Or you think bolder: making careful decisions to invest in adjacent businesses or new geographic markets. Edge strategy is the third way to explore growth opportunities that introduces opportunities in addition to those your core and noncore strategies might unearth.

Edges Are Everywhere

In searching for edges, we performed a rigorous analysis of some of the world's largest companies, canvassing the Standard & Poor's 500, the S&P Global 100, and the Global Dow.[13] Our work revealed that product edges were present, at least at a tactical level, in 45 percent of all companies studied. We identified journey edges in 30 percent and enterprise edges in 14 percent (see figure 1-4).[14]

However, while nearly all of the constituent industries we analyzed showed evidence of some sort of edge, the majority of companies within these sectors did not fully capitalize on the opportunities in their respective spaces.[15] We found a small group, approximately 10 percent of companies, that exhibits a consistent ability to find edges and to weave them into their corporate approach.[16] These "edge achievers" are also present in nearly every sector.

FIGURE 1-4

Edge tactics by type

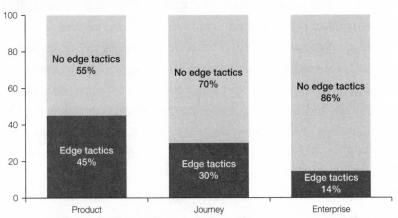

Percent of companies screened (N = 585*)

Source: Company websites and financials, trade press, and L.E.K. analysis.

*Excludes General Electric, Honeywell, Berkshire Hathaway, Leucadia, Dow Chemicals, DuPont Chemicals, 3M, Danaher, Roper Industries, BASF SE, Bayer, Hutchison Whampoa, Reliance Industries, ICBC, Koninklijke Philips, and Mitsui & Co.

FIGURE 1-5

Returns of edge achievers versus other companies

Source: Company websites and financials, S&P Capital IQ, L.E.K. analysis.

*Sharpe ratio calculated using monthly returns from 1/1/09–1/1/14. The Sharpe ratio is calculated as ((Average Portfolio Return - risk-free rate) / Portfolio Standard Deviation).

^Relative performance calculated as the unweighted average of (company performance / industry performance). Industry performance is unweighted. Only includes industries that contain edge achiever companies. This measure normalizes for inter-industry differences in revenue growth rates.

Note: Industries experiencing negative average growth during this time period were excluded from the CAGR analysis. Excludes: General Electric, Honeywell, Berkshire Hathaway, Leucadia, Dow Chemicals, Du Pont Chemicals, 3M, Danaher, and Roper Industries.

Interestingly, the edge achievers are also the winners. We estimate that these champions of edge strategy have increased risk-adjusted returns by more than 15 percent versus their peers. Furthermore, these companies have outgrown their peers by 39 percent (see figure 1-5).[17]

We are not asserting a direct causality, as edge strategy is necessarily incremental and is certainly not the only driver of these companies' success. We do find it striking, however, that those companies that have embraced edge strategy most fully are among those performing most strongly in their respective sectors. Edge strategy is indeed a habit of highly successful companies.

Our conclusion is that while edge opportunities are prevalent, companies do not maximize them. We suspect that this is due to a lack of awareness of the power that edges offer. Absent the right priorities and appropriate attention, and lacking the right mindset, it is hard to stumble on these opportunities by chance. The skill relies on recognizing patterns and asking the right questions.

The Structure of the Book

Half the battle with edges is being able to identify them, so the pattern-recognition metaphor is an apt one. You almost need peripheral vision, as this may involve a slightly different way of looking at your company. But, more than this, you need a new way of *thinking* about your company. You need what we call an "edge mindset." What you will get from this book is practice in identifying different types of opportunities, in different situations, and across different types of businesses. We hope some of these patterns will resonate with you and your own business.

With this goal in mind, we have arranged the book's content into two broad parts. The first part, "The Edge Framework and Mindset," describes the taxonomy of edge strategy and introduces an organizing framework that runs throughout the text. The second part, "Where to Unlock Value," applies the edge mindset to some common business challenges and shares our collective experience to guide you in harnessing the power of the edge in your business.

In chapter 2, we introduce product edge strategy. Product edges describe those situations in which your enterprise's product or service offering is imperfectly calibrated with some of your customers' needs. As a result, you have an opportunity to rescope the boundaries of your offer in order to better satisfy your customers' requirements. We use a simple framework to define the overlap between your offer and your customers' needs and demonstrate how misalignment can create a strategic opening for your business. The chapter also introduces two variants of product edge strategy—outside edges and inside edges—that we address in more detail in the second part of the book.

In chapter 3, we describe the second type of edge strategy—journey edges. We introduce the concept of the customer journey, which proposes that every customer interacts with your business as part of a larger mission extending beyond the four walls of your enterprise. Journey edges refer to those opportunities in which your enterprise is able to redefine its participation in helping complete that ultimate mission. Specifically, the redefinition requires expanding the company's solution to encompass the needs that either immediately precede or follow the core transaction. We study the example of Whole Foods, an organic grocer, whose prepared-foods category plays a critical role in completing its customers' mission of preparing a meal.

The first part concludes with chapter 4, in which we examine the third and final type of edge strategy, the enterprise edge. Enterprise edges, the most advanced form of edge strategy, can be found when the enterprise challenges the true utilization of its assets and unlocks value by leveraging those assets' latent potential in a new product-customer intersection.

These strategies are born from the fundamental question of "who, besides a direct competitor, would pay for the rights to any of my foundational assets?" We expand on this concept of foundational assets to illustrate how enterprise edge opportunities derive economic leverage by selling access to the foundational assets in a way that does not detract from the core offering. We conclude the chapter by taking you through three surprising case studies that illustrate the basic tenets of enterprise edge strategy.

In our treatment of all three types of edge strategy in the first part, we emphasize that they are incremental in effort, clearly leverage foundational assets, and are appended naturally to the core transaction as options. Furthermore, throughout these early pages, we have included an array of quantitative and descriptive evidence, collected from our comprehensive review of edge strategies across three major global equity indexes in order to further support our framework.

Chapter 5 begins the second part of the book by focusing on *effective upselling*. We discuss how you can use product and journey edge upselling to satisfy the customers' common desire of wanting something better. This type of edge-driven upselling is distinct from basic merchandising strategy (the well-worn "good, better, best" playbook); it encourages adoption of unique, separate add-on options that slightly redefine the customer-company relationship in a way that feels natural and makes the customer more satisfied.

The second half of the chapter offers a structure to help explain when and where upselling can be most effective. We profile six types of edge-based upselling and pair these with basic customer needs (convenience, comfort, relief, peace of mind, passion, and knowledge). We also use a detailed case study of a true upselling master—Royal Caribbean Cruise Lines—to extract some best practices. The chapter concludes with a discussion of how you can best present upselling options to your own customers.

Chapter 6 presents edge strategy in another practical context: *dealing with margin pressure*. The chapter begins by acknowledging an uncomfortable truth that faces many businesses: in all likelihood, some of your customers are unprofitable. It then tackles how edge strategy can correct the customer-profitability equation. A form of product edge strategy (the "inside edge") is particularly effective here; it allows you to "de-content" your offering so that the base version is more profitable for all customer segments, while simultaneously not alienating your most valuable customers. To reinforce this point, we use examples of how industries including airlines, gas stations, and medical devices have used this approach to maintain profitability in the face of stiff economic headwinds. The chapter concludes by discussing how a nonprofit deployed an inside edge strategy to mitigate the impact of budgetary pressure facing many public schools following the Great Recession.

Chapter 7 aims to help *combat commoditization*; specifically, it focuses on using edge strategy to drive marketing effectiveness. We discuss how to use options as a faster, less risky, less capital-intensive way to reposition products and sharpen differentiation. The chapter focuses on leveraging multiple product and journey edge strategies to communicate the value of ancillaries. We work stepwise through the application of an edge mindset to the otherwise familiar tools of customization, solutions, and bundling. The chapter concludes with a simple framework, the "edge merchandising matrix," that helps brings these concepts together holistically.

Chapter 8 discusses how the advent of *big data* has enabled edge strategy for many businesses. The exponential growth in the amount of data that businesses collect and use has created a challenge—and opportunity—for many. Companies that are using data to power their edge strategies are finding new and creative ways to create value; our research uncovered a broad range of emergent examples. This chapter surveys the various ways in which data can enable these edge plays and why many companies (not just cutting-edge technology firms) can monetize this value by renting access to more tech-savvy, sometimes unconventional users.

Chapter 9 begins by summarizing a well-known phenomenon: *mergers and acquisitions* often destroy value. We discuss how Imperial Chemical Industries PLC fell from a market cap of nearly $10 billion to complete dissolution in a decade. Given that deal success is commonly banked on the promise of new revenue, we advocate an edge-based perspective to validating these synergies. We demonstrate how the biotech industry has been more edge-oriented in its pursuit of deals than the big pharmaceutical companies and, in particular, how Gilead Sciences was able to string together highly accretive, edge-oriented deals. We use the example of Best Buy's Geek Squad to elucidate how deals themselves can sometimes be used to seed and accelerate edge strategy.

Finally, in chapter 10, we recapitulate our key learnings and present a ten-step process to identify and activate your edge strategy. It represents—in abridged form—the accumulated wisdom of our three decades of experience helping companies find their edge.

CHAPTER 2

EDGE OF THE PRODUCT

Rescoping the Boundaries of Your Offer

Our belief was that if we kept putting great products in front of customers, they would continue to open their wallets.

—*Steve Jobs, cofounder and CEO of Apple*

Arguably, no one was a better product strategist than Steve Jobs. For all that is written about the successes of Apple and the genius of its leader, the one common theme is Jobs's unfaltering focus on making great products. Designing products to completely and seamlessly meet the needs of customers was central to his strategy. It is also a key aspect of product edge strategy.

Customer centricity is not new. Many companies operate with a philosophy of listening to customers, trying to find gaps in the market, and designing solutions to fill these gaps. However, meeting the needs of your customer *entirely* is hard. First and foremost, it requires an ability to understand who your customer is.

Or more correctly who *they* are. The reality of virtually any market scenario is that there is not one homogeneous customer type. Every company attempts to serve a range of customers. The problem this causes for product design strategy is that it forces you to compromise on which customers you design your product for. Even if you can score a bull's-eye in producing a perfect product for those target customers, you inevitably end up serving many customers for whom your products or services are not perfectly aligned.

Product Edges

The edge of your product comprises its marginal aspects, the elements that have varying value to different customers. As we introduced in chapter 1, a way to think about your edge is to visualize a circle representing "your core offering" (see figure 2-1). The inside of the circle represents the sum of your product's features and benefits, and the edge of the circle reflects the perimeter of that product's scope. Take, for example, Apple's iPod. It is a digital music player; you can add music via Wi-Fi or a direct cable to a computer; it comes in various colors, sizes, and forms; it has various capacities for storage; it has a color screen; it can be bought online or in a store; it confers access to the iTunes library, and more. These are all features and elements of the same product offering.

If we draw a second circle to represent what your customers currently want from you, the edge of the circle frames what your customers give you permission to address in meeting their needs. We call this the "customer permission set" because it reflects what the customer is asking you to deliver. For example, it could be "I want a music player that can hold at least a thousand songs that I can carry in my pocket when I am jogging."

In an ideal world, the two circles would align perfectly, creating a kind of total eclipse (see figure 2-2). This would indicate that your offer is fully meeting your customers' needs.

FIGURE 2-1

Your company's core offering

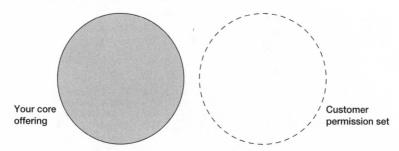

Your core strategy aims to align your commercial offering with your customers' set of needs.

FIGURE 2-2

Alignment of core offering and customer permission set

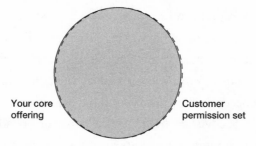

You are fully meeting customers' needs when the perimeter of your core offering eclipses the perimeter of where customers see value and therefore give you permission to serve.

In reality, this rarely happens. Even the target customers you focus on are not always fully satisfied with what they are buying. This could be because their needs have evolved since the product was originally designed. Alternatively, there could be shortcomings in the design itself, which is compounded when we factor in customer mix. We commonly find subsets of customers whose needs vary slightly or even materially from those of the archetypal customer to whom the base product is targeted. In these situations, the core offering does not align perfectly with customer needs either. The result of these misalignments is an opportunity for product edge strategies.

FIGURE 2-3

The outside edge of the core offering

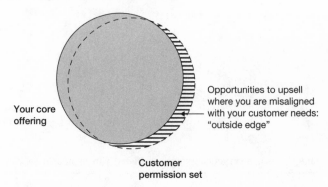

Your core offering

Opportunities to upsell where you are misaligned with your customer needs: "outside edge"

Customer permission set

Product edge opportunities exist when the perimeter of your core offering does not fully align with the permission set of your customers.

The most common form of product edge is what we call the "outside edge." Typically, your product is missing something that some customers really want. In every industry, some customers, even satisfied ones, tend to have some needs beyond what is met by the core offer. Put another way, they have needs that are just beyond the definition of our core offering: on the outside edge (see figure 2-3). To use the outside edge opportunity involves offering these customers enhancements to the core offer. These enhancements are typically priced and presented as add-ons or optional extras. The logic of this strategy plays directly to the heart of the idea we introduced at the start of this chapter: many customers will open their wallets wider if you can address their needs more precisely.

Apple's Edge

If you walked into one of the first two Apple Stores in late 2001 and purchased a brand-new iPod, you would have paid $399.[1] This product, originally launched that year with the slogan "1,000 songs in your pocket," was a clever combination of great design and the latest hardware components. This made it the smallest, most powerful and stylish personal music player yet. With it, you could upload from your Mac computer (the first version required that you own a Mac) nearly a hundred albums of music to carry around in your pocket, with up to ten hours of battery life.[2] Despite its considerable capabilities, your economic relationship with Apple didn't stop there. In fact, it had only just begun.

Buying the first iPod or any of the six generations that followed or the mini, nano, shuffle, and touch variants would have presented you with a set of options.[3] In addition to your music player, you may well have also purchased a case, or a charging mount, perhaps some mini speakers, headphones, or an extra cable to connect to your stereo. You may even have purchased an FM transmitter.[4]

These are all peripherals or accessories. Though none are essential to operating the iPod, all in some way provide incremental utility; they make the product more useful or just better. Apple manufactures some of these; for others, it licenses the rights to be labeled "brand compatible," but all are available as options in the Apple Store.[5]

This familiar story is full of product edges. The core product is the iPod, and the product edges are the broad range of add-ons that a consumer can purchase to meet specific needs. By licensing companies like Griffin and InCase to sell compatible accessories, Apple generated a high-margin, incremental revenue stream.[6] This stream required low investment and sat on top of the margin made on the core product. It was also low risk for Apple; allowing additional features like the FM transmitter to be sold as a third-party add-on meant that, if and when the technology becomes obsolete, Apple's core offer would be unaffected. But this was only the beginning of Apple's product edge strategy.

Apple has always been a hardware company. As figure 2-4 shows, approximately 90 percent of its revenue comes from its devices. With this perspective, Apple's music and video download service, iTunes, is another illustration of an outside product edge strategy in support of the core device offering.[7]

Apple generates about $13 per year in iTunes downloads per customer account.[8] The brilliance of iTunes is that it is a platform for

FIGURE 2-4

Apple's financial breakdown, 2014

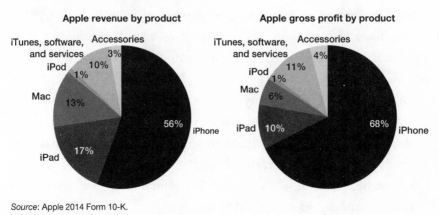

Source: Apple 2014 Form 10-K.

product edges, allowing Apple's customers to continuously buy add-ons that make the original product better. Every download is effectively an optional improvement to the original device purchase.

As Jobs explained, Apple gives the customer the ability to purchase optional add-ons to the original product that make it better. Customers respond by continuing to open their wallets again and again to recalibrate with their evolving needs. This is the essence of outside product edges; they consistently fulfill the following criteria:

- The add-on product (in this example, media content) is sold à la carte.

- The incremental effort for Apple is low (Apple has never ventured into producing music content; it merely acts as a channel).

- The leverage comes from foundational assets (in this case, the iTunes software platform and technology to load content onto its core devices).

- The return on investment from the above factors is substantial (for example, analysts estimate the operating margin on iTunes music and content is approximately 15 percent).[9]

Launched in July 2008, the App Store introduced yet another layer to Apple's edge story, and an even more powerful illustration: "apps."[10] Apple allows third parties to develop edge products for its core iPhone or iPad offerings and makes them available for purchase by its customers in the App Store. In exchange, Apple takes a percentage of all revenues.[11] Again, the apps in the store are optional add-ons to the mobile device, all of which provide incremental utility to a subset of customers for incremental charges.

While in iTunes the add-ons are content sourced from media companies, in the App Store the add-ons are often real functionality enhancements to the core product. They use the innovation and the creativity of others, catapulting the scale of options they can offer their customers. In both cases, the App Store and iTunes, Apple leverages the work of others to reduce its risk. If an app or song fails to gain traction, the cost to Apple is negligible. Again, Apple participates in every transaction in the App Store; this time the operating margin is estimated to be 46 percent.[12]

Even within the App Store itself, we find examples of product edges. If you were one of the more than five million daily players in 2014 to download the hugely successful "Clash of the Clans" game, you would find a typical feature of iOS games known as "in-app purchases."[13] The game is one in which players attempt to build a community, train troops, and attack other players to earn virtual gold, elixirs, and gems.[14] The game also allows players to pay real money (for example, $4.99 buys five hundred gems) to increase their virtual stockpiles while playing the game; these are in-app purchases and are unlimited.[15] This ability to buy add-ons and special features within an app is a standard model in the App Store. It is also the developer's outside product edge strategy. The core offering (an app) is sold or even given away for free in the App Store, but once the customer owns it, she is motivated to buy enhancements to better calibrate to her needs or permission set. Of course, Apple also has a role in provisioning this product edge, and it captures a percentage of these transactions as well.

In all these examples of Apple's outside product edges, we find the same pattern:

- There is an optional enhancement offered to a core product (add-on).

- The add-ons typically leverage foundational assets of the core business.

- The incremental effort and investment required to present and fulfill the enhancement is typically low.

- Incremental consideration is paid (extra charge) for this add-on.

Apple's many successes go well beyond edge strategy: there are, of course, many aspects to all winning market positions. What is clear is that the hallmarks of an edge mindset are present in nearly everything the company does.

The Inside Alternative

Thus far, we have explored how the misalignment of your core offering and a customer's permission set often creates enhancement opportunities. But this misalignment can also go in the opposite direction. Specifically, the misalignment might result not because the core offering is missing something, but rather because some customers do not universally value some elements of the core offering. While important for some customers, and perhaps even target customers, certain elements may not be valued by *all* customers. This is where we can find opportunities on the inside edge of the product (see figure 2-5).

If this type of inside edge exists in your business, you have an opportunity to do one of two things. First, you can unbundle the elements of your standard offer that are extraneous to some customer segments and sell them for an incremental fee only to those who value them.

FIGURE 2-5

The inside edge of the core offering

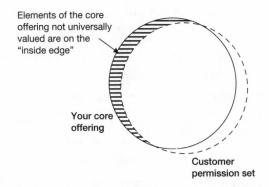

Elements of the core offering not universally valued are on the "inside edge"

Your core offering

Customer permission set

Inside edge opportunities exist when all customers do not universally value elements of the core.

Second, you can redefine the minimum standard product by shrinking or "de-contenting" it for everyone. Let's examine each in turn.

Unbundling the Product

With inside edge *unbundling*, you take an element of your offering that all customers do not value and parse it out as a separate option for an incremental charge. By doing this, you capture the value provided to the customers who do have a need for that element, while at the same time reducing the cost of providing it to those customers who don't value it.

Unbundling as a strategic concept is not new and has been applied in many industries. Some examples include unbundling legal services (when a lawyer provides support only for a discrete task such as reviewing a contract, instead of full representation) or unbundling software from computer systems (rather than selling a computer with an operating system installed, selling just the hardware).[16] The most typical form is *disassembly*, where the core offer is fundamentally broken down from a single offer into a new set of separate offers. When iTunes started selling all songs individually, it disassembled the previous core offer, the album (and changed how the industry operated).[17] This core strategy is not the subject of inside edges. Inside product edges rely on viable core offers but create opportunities to unbundle certain elements and offer them back to select customer sets as add-ons.

In 2008, US airlines realized that some people didn't need everything that they included in the sale of a standard airline ticket; this opened the door to unbundling elements of the "one size fits all" offer. Many travelers never check a bag, but historically their tickets subsidized the substantial cost for other travelers who often checked multiple bags. The airlines unbundled this element at the edge of their core offer, so today those who need the option pay for it.

"De-contenting:" When Less Is More

Inside edge *de-contenting* is the second way to exploit this phenomenon. Sometimes, the balance can tip so far that *more* of your customers are in the camp that doesn't value an element. In these cases, the best option might be to just do *less*.

In certain circumstances, customers can accept, if not welcome, simply removing or de-contenting the inside edge of your core offer. Usually, in the following situations, we see companies find success with this strategy:

- A majority of customers do not value the element.

- De-contenting can be positioned as a convenience, such as self-service.

- Some of the cost savings is shared in the form of a price reduction.

Familiar examples of this strategy in action are gas stations and retailers that have de-contented their labor models at the point of transaction to offer self-service versions of their core propositions. At one level, this gives customers the convenience of self-service and, in the case of gas stations, even some share of the cost savings.

More recently, companies have used de-contented offers in the health-care sector. Smith & Nephew and other medical device companies have responded to cost challenges in the US health-care industry with de-contented options. Smith & Nephew offers "rep-less" orthopedic implants; a hospital can purchase (for a reduced fee) a replacement knee or hip as a device-only option, without the support of a sales representative. As with gas station self-service, this solution appeals to a subset of customers who are comfortable with reduced service. Like gas stations, the rep-less implant customer also shares in some of the cost savings through a reduced overall price.

A common theme among examples of inside edges, both unbundling and de-contenting, is that both are useful in combating various types of pressure on profit margins. They are often manifested during structural discontinuities at an industry level. Unavoidable challenges such as escalating oil prices, a collapse in overall demand, or structural changes to reimbursement models are all examples where companies have been prompted to explore opportunities at the inside edge of their products. In chapter 6, we will explore these examples in further detail to understand the effectiveness of this approach.

Next, we describe the second type of edge strategy: the journey edge.

CHAPTER 3

EDGE OF THE JOURNEY

Completing the Customer's Mission

We're more than just a grocery store;
we're a restaurant and a premier brand.

—John Mackey, founder and co-CEO, Whole Foods

One of the greatest success stories over the last two decades has been the growth of Whole Foods Market. The grocer's share performance increased over 3,000 percent between 1994 and 2014, more than eight times the return of the corresponding S&P 500 index.[1] Many factors contributed to this: an innovative concept, premium positioning in an organic food supertrend, and, critically, a philosophy of partnering with customers in their broader "journeys." This last point, the premise behind journey edges, is the subject of this chapter.

The Journey Analogy

Edge strategy acknowledges that the boundaries defined by a product do not typically mark the beginning and end of the journeys that initially prompted customers to engage. These journeys often start before a company actually sees the customer and tend to continue well after they have transacted.

Let's start with the most literal of examples and think about all the steps of a real journey. If someone was traveling from New York City to Los Angeles on a business trip, an airline would have a very narrow lens on that customer's actual purpose. Despite multiple touch points at check-in, airport security, boarding, flight, and baggage claim, the airline would draw false conclusions about the customer's objectives based solely on its own interactions. To get a complete picture, we need to think through all the steps. The customer might have planned the trip through an online travel agency, purchased a new travel bag, and parked her car at an airport lot before the airline even saw her. After she left the airline's sight, she might have taken a taxi, checked into a hotel, and then met with a client for dinner. If the customer's end mission was actually to make a big sale to her client, what a distorted picture the airline would have by inferring that her mission was simply to take a flight!

What an airline offers that passenger may actually change if it knows the true purpose, or mission, of her journey. The preoccupied businesswoman on her way to make the big sale is certainly going to be in a different mindset than the retiree sitting to her left returning home to his spouse, or the college student on her right on his way to spring break. They will all have different pain points and very different needs leading up to, and exiting, the airline's care.

Opening the aperture further allows us to see the whole journey for what it really is: a much longer sequence of events involving multiple transactions across a variety of partners before a desired outcome is achieved. Setting aside our trip analogy, we can recognize figurative "journeys" in almost every type of business. Customers of nearly every product or service seek to achieve an end, an end that is typically much bigger (to them) than the actual transaction. They, too, are on a sort of mission, and products merely help in this endeavor. Does a customer buy a flat-screen TV because he wants to own an electronic device? Or rather because he wants to sit on his couch and consume entertainment? Is the mission of a trip to the grocery store the acquisition of items for the pantry? Or might the underlying mission be a hot meal for the family?

Occasionally, customers see a product as helping complete an entire mission. More often, customers view products as simply playing a role in a larger effort that involves other steps (and other products or services) to achieve the mission. The end-to-end set of steps required to reach a customer's ultimate mission is what we call, figuratively, the "customer journey." Most companies intersect with only a subset of steps in a journey, implying that the portion of the journey a company overlaps has its own edges. A journey edge demarks that portion of a customer journey (to achieve some mission) that a company currently sees.

But is this level of participation fixed? Customer journeys often have frustrations and frictions. Sometimes, customers simply lack a good map of where they are going. If, in a natural and complementary way, you can walk just a couple of steps further with your customer toward the completion of his or her mission, then you likely have a journey edge.

Extending the Framework

Thinking in terms of journeys encourages you to expand solutions, to encompass needs that immediately precede or follow the core transaction. Finding journey edges involves asking the question: *What mission is my customer ultimately hoping to accomplish with my product and would he or she give me permission to help more toward this end?*

Returning to the framework we introduced in chapter 2, let's assume that your core offering does a pretty good job approximating the customer permission set. You don't have a perfect eclipse, and indeed there is some work to do around the edges of your product, but your

FIGURE 3-1

Customer mission space

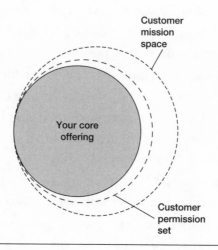

offer is more or less what your customers expect from you. Now, let's think about things in the more holistic context of the customer journey. We can imagine another broad circle, surrounding the customer permission set, which represents what the customer ultimately wants to accomplish on her journey (see figure 3-1). This circle we call the "customer mission space" since it represents a broader objective for which your product is merely a stepping-stone.

The customer permission set that you are trying to address is smaller than the customer mission space that is required to complete the customer's journey. Maybe your customer historically never thought you could be of further help. Maybe you just never thought to ask if you could walk a couple more steps along her journey. Either way, there is an opportunity to redefine your current participation along the edge of the current customer permission set (see figure 3-2). If your customer lets you help with a little more, at the fringe of what you do already, then you have found an opportunity at the journey's edge.

As we discussed in chapter 2, product edges question the sufficiency of a single product boundary in a world of diverse customer needs.

FIGURE 3-2

The journey edge

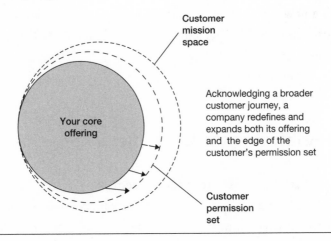

Customer
mission
space

Acknowledging a broader
customer journey, a
company redefines and
expands both its offering
and the edge of the
customer's permission set

Your core
offering

Customer
permission
set

Product edges imply that enhancements, or optional features, are required to satisfy different customers. Journey edges go a step further, challenging the premise that *any variant* of your product is adequate. In order to satisfy the more broadly defined, underlying need, you must begin to append not just attributes, but additional (highly synergistic) products or services to your core product.

An important aspect of journey edges is that they remain, in fact, edges. By contrast, vertical integration strategies often tend to go well beyond our definition. Vertical integration contemplates moving outside the core business into completely new stages of a value chain. While capturing upstream or downstream margin might be a worthy goal, it has a very different risk profile from moving only slightly further along a customer journey. Vertical integration often requires significant development or acquisition of brand-new assets and capabilities. The majority of what you need to make vertical integration successful is typically not present when you commence the strategy.

For this same reason, ventures that require investing into a separate, adjacent space also rarely qualify as edges. Journey edges are distinct from these bolder strategies because they are incremental in nature: expanding slightly on permission that already exists versus seeking to establish a new permission. Said another way, they are highly complementary to the core offering, and so the foundational assets that enable them should largely already be present.

Analyzing the Customer's Endgame

Many ancillary businesses that today seem almost core at one time started out as journey edges. For example, retailers often augment sales with accompanying support such as assembly or installation services. Think of a home goods retailer selling an unassembled outdoor grill as a box of parts and leaving its customer's mission incomplete. When that retailer also sells assembly and delivery, it takes another step in the journey to the customer's true mission of cooking in his backyard. Another example is the business-to-business service contracts that are layered on top of software sales. Maintenance, installation, training, delivery, anything at all that turns do-it-yourself into a do-it-for-me solution originally resulted from exploring the edge of where core products intersect with customer journeys.

Let's take an example from Colfax, a multibillion-dollar industrial products company.[2] Its ESAB division—with manufacturing facilities throughout Central and Eastern Europe, South America, and Asia—is one of the world's leading manufacturers of welding consumables and equipment.[3] Welding guns and TIG torches, as well as the consumable filler used to enable the tools, are the company's core business.[4] However, the company also has a robust edge strategy. Along with these products, ESAB provides, at the edge of its core product business, many related services. These include welding education, product training, and value-added engineering (consulting) assistance.[5] Some of these are revenue streams, and others, as we will see in chapter 7, are bundled with the product to sell larger solutions. In either case, the company has made choices about moving, just incrementally, beyond the sale of product and closer to the customer's end mission. ESAB's approach, like the discovery of all journey edges, essentially boils down to four steps.

Step 1: Customer Segmentation

First, segment customers based on their ultimate missions and the journeys required to get them there. The practical implication is to create manageable customer clusters, each of which can be addressed similarly. As was the case in our literal journey, the trip from New York City to Los Angeles, different customers use products differently, depending on their ultimate missions.

In ESAB's case, let's imagine examples of two customer archetypes. In reality, there would be many more customer missions within a number of different customer segments, but for illustration, let's stick to a simple two-customer example. The first customer is a procurement manager for a fabricated metal factory that is buying more welding filler (consumables) to replace depleted inventory. The second customer is a foreman for a large oil rig whose mission is the completion of a large episodic repair. Let's also assume that each of these customers is pursuing essentially the same transaction, say, a big order of welding filler. However, each has a very different ultimate mission and, in turn, journey to get there. Likewise, the filler transaction plays a very different role in both journeys.

Step 2: Mission Definition

The next step is to clearly and specifically articulate the mission each customer segment seeks. This sounds easy enough, but in reality requires a certain detached objectivity that looks beyond the features of the product and into the psyche of the customer. Before a company can possibly determine where it can go one step beyond its existing offering, it needs to deeply investigate what the customer *really* wants.

In the case of the first ESAB customer, the procurement manager at the fabricated metal factory has a mission of keeping the filler in stock to maintain a metal-bending process without interruption. In this instance, ESAB's product sales are sufficient to cover most of a relatively simple mission. For the second customer, the oil rig foreman, the mission is much broader and the welding materials themselves are almost an afterthought. He needs to buy enough welding filler to complete a onetime job, but the real mission is the completion of a major repair on the oil rig. This different mission drives a very different view about the transaction; the oil rig foreman is completely focused on solving an expensive problem, and the cost of the filler is relatively trivial.

Step 3: Journey Mapping

The next step is to work backward from the missions to map out in detail the journey that each customer segment takes to reach them. This is a rigorous process; it involves meticulously moving step-by-step from the moment the customer identified his broader mission until the time he has completed it.

Keeping with our example, the factory procurement manager must ensure that proper maintenance material is on hand. This means that the simple supply of ESAB's product covers, say, 80 percent of the manager's journey. However, ESAB doesn't *complete* the journey, as the manager must continue to monitor inventory and decide when he needs to reorder. Therefore, the edge of the journey that ESAB addresses could conceivably be expanded slightly, if ESAB was extended the permission to provide this additional inventory management service.

In the case of the oil rig foreman, the supply of materials is only a small part, say 20 percent, of the ultimate mission. With the oil rig, ESAB is providing only a stepping-stone on a much more involved journey. This second journey has many steps, both before and after the product is acquired. The full journey begins with identifying the problem, specifying the repair, and determining the supplies required prior to any interaction with ESAB. After buying the filler from ESAB, the oil rig would also have to retain temporary help and possibly train and

TABLE 3-1

Incremental moves for two missions

Customer	Permission set (initial)	Mission space	Journey edge opportunity	Percent of journey addressed by initial permission	Percent of journey addressed after edge strategy
Procurement manager, fabricated metal factory	Sale of filler	Adequate inventory maintenance	Inventory management service	80% ➡	90%
Foreman, oil rig	Sale of filler	Completed major welding repair job	Training and consulting on usage of welding supplies	20% ➡	30%

supervise its own staff to accomplish the actual welding required for the repair. More importantly, the oil rig foreman is probably more than amenable to paying for any required support to get his oil rig up and running again. Clearly, these two different missions create different journey edges that can be accessed across the two segments.

Many of the steps in the second journey might be too far afield to contemplate as edge strategies. Actually doing the welding repairs would take ESAB into a much riskier adjacent space. However, consulting, training, and instructing on the application of the tools it is already selling—these are edges, the incremental moves for which the majority of foundational assets are already in place. Knowing the whole journey map helps ESAB understand more intuitively where the lower-risk edges are, and where it might be able to play (see table 3-1).

Step 4: Permission Testing

Finally, determine exactly where customers would give you permission to do more. This is critical. In many cases, you simply might not be credible in offering one of the subsequent steps. Maybe some steps are already well served. Perhaps expanding an offer in certain dimensions would seem unnatural or disjointed. However, if you can provide these steps more cheaply or more effectively than the customer could achieve with alternatives, a journey edge opportunity is possible.

In the case of ESAB, the edge is product support marketed as services. This service includes live consultation with customers to whom the company supplies product. Productivity assessments, profitability analysis, and improvement proposals are examples of items wrapped into consulting solutions that aim to improve customers' performance.[6] ESAB could charge for these as incremental edge revenue streams or choose to bundle them as a means to secure larger contracts.

The key is that the knowledge to provide these services already resides within ESAB. The ability to diagnose opportunities is facilitated because ESAB already provides the systems, tools, and consumables to its existing customers. Its intimate customer knowledge is itself a key asset that can be leveraged in addressing a journey edge opportunity. As a matter of course, the leverage from foundational assets is the best angle into participating in additional steps in a journey.

In many cases, we find that journey edges can be tested in advance. Just because your offer does not reside within the existing customer permission set does not mean that it couldn't. Dialoguing with customers can answer questions of where they need more help and where they view your company as a potential partner. Either way, moving incrementally is important. The very thing that makes a journey edge an "edge" is that you already have most of what is required to service the additional need. The very same characteristics that make journey edges high leverage and low risk should also increase the odds that you would be credible in servicing the additional step.

Whole Foods Market's Winning Edge

When Whole Foods Market was founded in Texas in 1978, there was no evidence that the company would eventually be serving sit-down meals to diners. Back then, it was a classic grocery business, albeit specialized in organic products.[7] Over the ensuing period, however, what was originally a deli counter expanded into a vast array of premium services in the form of ready-to-eat options.[8] Sushi bars, barbecue stands, Mexican food stations, and espresso bars are now backed by professional chefs and an attentive support staff that clears tables and keeps a sit-down dining area spotless. How did this come to pass?

Whole Foods is a remarkable example of a company that recognized the journey edges in its business. The company then used value-added services as a means to expand its relationship at or near these edges. Whole Foods explicitly describes this approach to the market. Referring to journeys as customer "modes," the co-chief operating officer, A. C. Gallo, told Wall Street analysts that Whole Foods' strategy was to configure its offer to accommodate these different customer missions. According to Gallo, "One mode is 'I want to just get ingredients.' Another mode is 'I want to get something already partially prepared I can take home and finish.' And another is 'I want to get things already cooked.'"[9]

Whole Foods already possessed many of the foundational assets required to build a prepared foods business. It already had stores and foot traffic. It had relationships with customers and was able to capitalize on existing interactions in a natural way. Whole Foods also enjoyed a strong supply chain with gourmet, organic ingredients (with far better buying power than most hospitality companies). The move did need some investing in prep kitchens and building a section, sometimes on a second floor, to accommodate diners.[10] But it only required marginal changes to the labor model. Overall, the initiative was much more efficient and effective than what a third party starting a similar greenfield concept could accomplish.

The results of this journey edge strategy are staggering. In 2014, Whole Foods boasted sales of $2.7 billion in prepared foods and bakery—accounting for about 20 percent of the company's revenues.[11] Industry gross profit margins from prepared foods are typically 55 percent, which is one-and-a-half times what Whole Foods realizes in its overall business.[12] We see this phenomenon repeatedly. If a complementary system is constructed appropriately, the core business enables an ancillary business to earn the outsized margins that power the company.

What makes this a quintessential journey edge strategy is that prepared foods were a natural extension of what Whole Foods was providing for customers on a day-to-day basis. The new business was more than related; it was directly complementary to the core. Moreover, the edge characteristics of the business were never lost on founder John Mackey. He let the world know that he was not interested in extending Whole Foods' brand into an adjacent food service space. "Let me be clear that we do not want to open fast-food restaurants," he once told analysts. "We are food retailers, and we've got a great strategy, and as you can see, we're producing great results. I think we ought to stick with it and not get distracted."[13]

A Chinese Journey

There are many potential journey edge applications. In our analysis of hundreds of global companies, we found that nearly 30 percent exercised a journey edge of some sort.[14] A combination of strategies and tactics, the most common manifestations could loosely be called types of consulting (17 percent), training (15 percent), and installation (8 percent).[15] We have also found examples of journey edges in many different countries. The powerful idea to slightly reframe the customer relationship through ancillary options is culturally agnostic and pervades geographical boundaries.

Take another example, on the other side of the world from Whole Foods headquarters, in Shenzhen, China.[16] Colour Life, a publicly listed company on the Hong Kong exchange, is one of China's leading property management companies.[17] In 2014 the company managed more than five hundred residences (apartment complexes) across China.[18] The company's relevant foundational assets were a centralized and automated property management system, a direct presence in each of its residences, and, most importantly, a large tenant base.[19]

Colour Life initially had two core business lines. One, property management itself, includes such things as security, gardening, cleaning, repair, and maintenance. The second, engineering services, includes equipment leasing, installation, and maintenance. However, Colour Life distinguished itself by introducing a third line aimed at improving its residents' quality of life. The company did this by providing online and offline service platforms for residents, where qualified local vendors could promote their own services and products.[20]

The company realized that its customers had many unmet needs that began right where its relationship officially ended. It also recognized that a host of vendors were eager to provide just these services to its clientele. To provide the services directly would require a risky step into unfamiliar adjacent businesses. But to *facilitate* the deals, lubricating transactions, was right at the edge of what Colour Life was already doing.

The insight was that customers were not merely renting maintained space; they were making homes. As such, they needed everyday conveniences such as fresh groceries, cut flowers, decorations, household item repairs, and anything normally associated with the upkeep of apartments. A vendor network would allow residents to quickly and conveniently get help with a variety of steps along the journey of residency.

The innovation was to create both digital and physical marketplaces for vendors to sell these goods to their tenants and liberally deploy foundational assets. The company leveraged existing community centers to provide bricks-and-mortar space for local vendors. Online, it built a purchase platform for locally sourced basic necessities. This online solution utilized its existing centralized network operations center, an investment originally used to make more efficient use of labor forces for certain services.[21]

"Community leasing, sales, and other services" is the third business line where Colour Life reports its edge revenue. Altogether, it is about 17 percent of the company's revenue.[22] The bottom-line impact is where the edge-based leverage shows up. Average property management profit margins in China tend to run between 5 percent and 10 percent. By comparison, Colour Life's profit margins averaged approximately 30 percent in the three years ending in 2014.[23]

Where Journeys Begin and End

A final, intriguing characteristic of journey edges is that they tend to present themselves even if you do nothing to enable them. Companies commonly discount this evidence as a special case. In fact, some companies end up giving away their edge, not realizing the potential they are squandering.

If a business is at, or pretty close to, the actual beginning or end of the customer's journey, then odds are there is no partner assisting with the initiation or completion of the mission. In these cases, the customer often seeks counsel from whoever is closest to this step of the journey. The interactions we witness at the beginning of journeys often involve such things as scoping options, designing a solution, or assessing the economic feasibility of a job to be done. Salespeople might do some of this for free, just to close the core sale. Likewise, at the end of journeys, we see interactions in extending product life, reconfiguration, and product disposal. We think these are a great place to look for opportunity.

As we will see in chapter 9, the consumer electronics giant Best Buy is a great example that underscores this point. The company built "Geek Squad," a technical service team, which was seeded initially by a small acquisition and was focused on taking the next step of its customers' journey after purchase. When someone buys a home theater system, it needs to be installed, and Geek Squad can do that for a charge. As a computer ages, it often develops problems that need troubleshooting and fixing: Geek Squad can do that, too. With a Geek Squad desk in the corner of the store, Best Buy's edge is to sell one more step of the journey to as many customers as possible. As we will see in chapter 9, the strategy was very successful.

But how did Best Buy know to move into this business in the first place? Was it a guess? A simple juxtaposition of double-digit service margins with the razor-thin profits of "selling boxes," with hope that it would work? The answer really surprised us.

The company, given its strong sales and customer service culture, was already active in ancillary services; it just wasn't charging for them. Sales associates were helping customers with in-store installation of batteries and disc drives. They were helping customers identify complementary auxiliary items (that the company often did not sell) to facilitate home solutions. When a few customers returned to the store with a postpurchase issue, associates were helping to troubleshoot. None of these ad hoc services was high volume and, as a result, remained largely unnoticed. However, there was evidence that (1) many product sales were insufficient to complete their respective journeys, (2) customers clearly needed help with these steps, and (3) customers would give Best Buy permission to assist.

When Best Buy, one by one, turned its normal stores into Geek Squad–enhanced stores, it imposed a formality that previously did not exist. By hanging stock-keeping units and prices on activities, Best Buy was enabling income from activities that were happening in small volume already. By no longer giving away the edge, Best Buy simply changed how many customers could enjoy these intuitively complementary services and built a process to deliver them more consistently.

EDGE OF THE ENTERPRISE

Viewing Your Assets from the Outside

If you're watching live video on the internet, there's a good chance [Major League Baseball Advanced Media] is involved. MLBAM streams more live video than any other sports entity—and any other company.

—*Ben Stricker, senior PR manager, Cisco Unified Computing System*

Enterprise edges are the third form of edge strategy, and while they can often be the hardest to recognize, they can also be the most accretive. Product and journey edges adopt a customer's slightly broader perspective of how your business fits its needs; by contrast, enterprise edges require viewing your business from the vantage point of a complete outsider. What can I do with what I already have? It sounds like an obvious question that most companies are equipped to answer. As we shall detail in this chapter, the unexpected answers to this question, answers that seem perpendicular to everyday business, often characterize enterprise edges. Let us start by considering the notion of an enterprise edge in its most basic, elemental form.

Harvesting at the Farm's Edge

For many generations, farmers have relied on wind to pump water and power other activities.[1] But today, it is not only farmers who exploit the wind on farmlands. Farms now rent out the vast open space on their properties to developers. These developers, in turn, construct wind turbines to harness the latent energy potential that happens to already exist in the air above the fields.[2] This is a great example of an enterprise edge strategy.

Someone thought to ask the key question: "Who, besides a direct competitor, would pay for rights to my land?" One answer is an energy company. At its simplest level, wide open fields in Kansas provide highly attractive real estate to support a wind farm. With minimal burden and little risk to its core business, a farm can lease the rights to build windmills above its crops, powering generators and driving a new revenue stream at the edge of its farming enterprise. "I think it's one of the greatest things that ever happened," said Chuck Goodman, a retired farmer from New Alta, Iowa. "It's good for my pocketbook. It's good for the environment. And wind is renewable; we're not digging it out of a hole in the ground."[3]

Wind leases typically provide farmers with annual payments ranging between $4,000 and $8,000 per turbine, plus additional royalty payments of 3 percent to 6 percent of gross revenues.[4] Farmers are selling access to a key asset (their land) to a new customer base (wind developers) with minimal disruption to their core business (raising crops). The land sits at the base of a farm's stack of foundational assets; its core purpose is to enable the growth of crops, but when viewed through another lens, it offers much additional potential.

As with product and journey edges, exploiting enterprise edges requires little incremental investment; in this case, the land already existed to serve the core business. Unlocking latent potential at the edge of the enterprise also serves a new customer permission set in a way that doesn't interfere with the core business.

Where Are Enterprise Edges Found?

We have already introduced the concept of the enterprise as a stack of foundational assets. Enterprise edges tend to be found lying along the periphery of all of these foundational assets (see figure 4-1). Importantly, all of the assets that support your core offering have edges of their own.

Any foundational asset could, at its edge, unlock an opportunity. Sometimes, an asset that directly supports your core can *coincidentally* support the majority of what is needed to satisfy a completely different

FIGURE 4-1

Edge of the enterprise

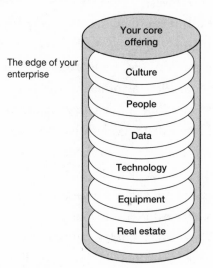

Enterprise edge opportunities exist when you explore how your company's edge extends across its foundational assets.

customer permission set. This coincidence is an important distinction. What characterizes the thinking behind this third type of edge strategy is the recognition that the new way of using or deploying your asset is already close to a useful solution for the new customer. Your organization also requires little incremental effort to present this new solution to the new customer.

Opportunities for incremental growth exist in any situation in which you can challenge the true utilization of foundational assets. If you can unlock additional utility by leveraging a foundational asset's potential to serve a new product-to-customer intersection without affecting the core business, it is an edge of the enterprise opportunity. Most fundamentally, finding an enterprise edge opportunity involves asking and exploring the answers to the question our farmers asked of themselves: *Who, besides a direct competitor, would pay for the rights to any of my foundational assets?*

Growth initiatives for which your organization has inadequate experience, knowledge, or relationships are typically not candidates for prioritization. However, enterprise edges are atypical.

Unlike traditional forays into new customers or new products, significant risk taking or investment is not necessary to exploit enterprise edge opportunities. Instead, they involve recognizing the latent value in your assets if you make them accessible to another organization. As such, executing on enterprise edge opportunities is primarily about connecting others with, or allowing others to access, your existing assets.

Often, this starts by selling limited usage rights for one of your foundational assets to a player that previously had no interaction with this part of your business. This allows you to monetize the opportunity without disrupting, or adding undue complexity to, your core. You may have amassed assets that support your core business that you can rent out profitably (to other companies) in a way that poses no threat to your commercial viability. These assets could be tangible, say, a factory or a piece of machinery, or they could be intangible, say, capabilities or relationships.

An enterprise edge opportunity may be present with an intangible asset, such as data (see figure 4-2). The company can align its

FIGURE 4-2

Example of enterprise edge opportunity

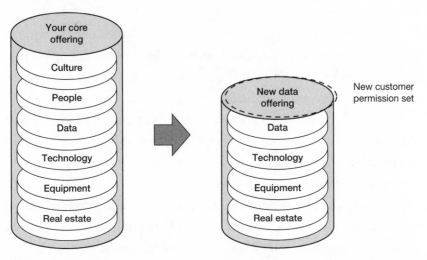

When you can recognize how one of your foundational assets can readily fulfill the needs of a new customer, you create enterprise edge opportunities.

foundational asset with an entirely new customer permission set, one completely distinct from the customer permission set of its core offering.

Consider a highly transactional organization such as a health insurance company, constantly processing transactions, claims, and payments for its thousands of customers. In doing so, the health insurer will amass vast amounts of data about its customers and their health. This data is a storybook on how its customers live and respond to care, which, if presented appropriately, would provide insight to companies that also provide care to those customers. (See the example of UnitedHealth in the next section.)

Enterprise edge opportunities become manifest in many forms, yet they all leverage foundational assets in one of three ways:

- Monetizing by-products

- Unlocking latent capacity

- Exploiting unconstrained or intangible assets

Let us now consider each form in turn.

Monetizing By-products

By finding new ways to harvest the full value of your output, you can monetize by-products. You can find the most obvious example in the by-products of your core business, the material left over from—or created by—the process of producing your core goods and services. While the wind energy example may be a new opportunity for farmers, they are no strangers to enterprise edges. Using by-products of one activity to support another is standard practice in farming, for example, feeding cornstalks to dairy cows.[5]

There are also many industrialized examples where enterprise edges are commonplace. For example, in the oil-refining industry, gasoline production generates a number of by-products, such as hydrogen. A typical oil refinery sells and processes these by-products, or "intermediates," into additional products at colocated chemical processing plants.[6]

These activities are, of course, well-established industry norms. The value of the enterprise edge framework is to provide a mindset that can help us see these opportunities for what they are, even though they are not parallel with our core operations. A good illustration of a modern and less traditional use of by-products is UnitedHealth's efforts to monetize its data assets.

As the largest health insurer in the United States, UnitedHealth has a core business that generated revenues of $113.9 billion in 2014: the selling and managing of health insurance to individuals and employers, as well as to the government via the Medicare and Medicaid programs.[7] UnitedHealth also operates a smaller business called OptumInsight that provides its customers with information culled from the enormous database that the parent company has developed to track health outcomes in its core insurance business.[8] This is an enterprise edge business—one that serves drug companies.

OptumInsight was founded in 1996 under another name: Ingenix.[9] As analysts noted at the time, the business "builds upon the company's database and expertise in providing knowledge and information services."[10] Here we see the familiar characteristics of an enterprise edge opportunity. In pursuit of its core business, UnitedHealth built a considerable data trove that is more broadly valuable than what could be exploited by its core alone. It recognized that due to the nature of data, it could readily leverage this foundational asset elsewhere without significant new investment. It also recognized that it could generate incremental cash flow without affecting its core business.

With more than 80 million people using its insurance products, and with a collection of patient information on 114 million people dating back to 1993, UnitedHealth claims to have "one of the largest and most robust proprietary healthcare databases in the world."[11] For the drug companies, the patient-specific, longitudinal nature of the data set (that is, the fact that it tracks the outcomes of patients over time), together with its geographic diversity, is hugely valuable. OptumInsight developed a suite of products that allow the drug companies to use this data for their own purposes, which is quite separate from UnitedHealth's core business.[12]

One of the tools—offered under the brand name Clinformatics—is called "Data Mart." This online tool, providing anonymized or "de-identified" information on patients, is designed to help drug companies understand how their products (and those of their rivals) are used by and perform for customers. In its promotional literature, UnitedHealth urges companies to "see how a greater depth of knowledge can help you reduce research and development costs, shorten go-to-market time-lines and maintain quality and compliance."[13]

The edge insight was that nearly everything required to power a new offering—in this case, the data—was already present within the enterprise. So while it is typically a step into the risky unknown to target new customers in a new sector, enterprise edges represent a special case; risk is heavily mitigated because much of the new offering already exists. All that remains is to make it available to the customers who value it.

OptumInsight's overall revenue figures suggest that their new customers see the value. In 2014 the division generated $5.2 billion—up from $956 million in 2006.[14] Over this time, its annual growth rate, 16 percent, was more than three times the growth rate for United-Health as a whole (7 percent).[15] Its profitability is even more impressive. In 2014, OptumInsight earned $1 billion in operating income—a 19 percent margin. By contrast UnitedHealth, as a whole, reported $10.3 billion—an 8 percent margin.[16] By any measure, OptumInsight has grown over time to become a core business for UnitedHealth. Sometimes edge strategies can evolve into robust profit centers that transcend the original incremental opportunity.

Unlocking Latent Capacity

Finding creative means to release any of the resources or capabilities in your stack of foundational assets unlocks latent capacity. Many enterprises build capabilities to produce and/or deliver their core products. Often these are vast and complex assets: production plants, infrastructure networks, data centers, and so on, where an opportunity can sometimes be found in their spare capacity.

As with by-products, monetizing spare capacity is commonplace for some industries. For example, many manufacturing and production companies, such as brewing, food processing, even pharmaceuticals, rent out spare production capacity or offer toll manufacturing services.[17] However, we have also found examples of companies using the same edgelike thinking that spawned these standard practices in less obvious situations. Just as with the more conventional manufacturing examples, these businesses also recognized ways to create incremental revenue streams by renting out spare capacity that would have otherwise gone unused. Some examples include seasonal call centers that handle customer service for other companies during the off-season and universities that rent out meeting spaces for private events outside of term.[18]

An excellent illustration of this kind of edge strategy is Major League Baseball's discovery that it could effectively deploy its streaming video capabilities for other broadcasters and content providers during baseball's off-season. When you watch Clayton Kershaw throw a pitch at Dodger Stadium in Los Angeles or see Miguel Cabrera hit a home run at Comerica Park in Detroit, chances are you are catching a live streaming of the game on your laptop, tablet, or smartphone. Every one of the three hundred or so pitches in a game, every one of the twenty-five hundred games in a season, are now readily available on any device, wherever you are.[19]

This service is brought to you not by a traditional broadcaster but by Major League Baseball's (MLB) own media business: Major League Baseball Advanced Media (MLBAM). Set up in 2000, at the height of the dot-com boom, this company, which is jointly owned by the thirty clubs in the league, was tasked with running the websites of the MLB and its different clubs.[20] But, in the intervening fifteen years, it has branched out and become a pioneer in the business of streaming live video content online worldwide.

Early on, the narrow focus was on how the league and the clubs could improve their websites with the pooled resources of the various clubs. Each invested just $2.6 million, creating a total fund of $77 million. "Centralizing these activities means that we have more money to build state-of-the-art technology," reflected Bob Bowman, the company's CEO. Also, by orchestrating a collaborative effort, MLB ensured that super-rich teams—such as the New York Yankees or the Boston Red Sox—would not break away and establish their own digital operations. It "means that the fan in Milwaukee is going to get the same great site as the fan in New York," Bowman explained.[21]

Soon MLBAM was entering a new world of digital technology— leading the way with not just website management but also app development and video streaming. In 2008 it debuted its "NexDef" feature, downloadable software for high-quality streaming of video on widescreen formats. The following year, MLBAM launched a new video player with high-definition pictures, the functionality of digital video recorders, multigame viewing options, live game highlights, and a player tracker.[22]

By this time, MLBAM was attracting more than 50 million unique visitors to its websites every month. Among these, there were 1.5 million subscribers to its multimedia content—including five hundred thousand people who paid $100 or more for access to MLB. TV, the flagship video product.[23]

Yet, for nearly half the year, during baseball's off-season from October to March, the company was less productive than it could have been. When viewed through a more expansive lens, there was significant theoretical capacity trapped in the system it had built for its own needs.[24] The banks of computers and other digital infrastructure occupied nearly eight thousand square feet at the company's Manhattan headquarters, but they were underused during the winter months.[25] MLBAM realized that the assets it had built to serve its core business, its technology, and its people could be leveraged to capture an entirely new income stream. Recognizing this edge opportunity set the stage for a remarkable success story.

In March 2010, ESPN, the television sports channel, announced it would contract with MLBAM to stream all of its online content.[26] In ten years, MLBAM had leaped past traditional broadcasters in the delivery of live web-based content and, by renting out its spare capacity, had found a lucrative opportunity at the edge of its core business. The league and the clubs had recouped their investment in the company after only seven years, so all the activity after this was hugely profitable.[27] In 2014, MLBAM's revenue was approaching $800 million.[28] Of this, about $50 million came from its edge customers, ESPN and a host of other clients, including CBS, World Wrestling Entertainment, and even the latest Guns N' Roses world tour.[29]

In 2005, Major League Baseball had considered spinning off MLBAM. At the time, its putative value was $2.5 billion.[30] Today, with the fast-growing "edge of the enterprise" business helping to boost the number of live events from ten thousand in 2011 to thirty thousand in 2014, the company is almost certainly worth considerably more.[31]

Exploiting Unconstrained
or Intangible Assets

The most expansive form of enterprise edge is found in the exploitation of unconstrained or intangible assets. In some circumstances, the enterprise has developed an asset that is so easily scalable that a company can leverage it elsewhere in a way that is unlimited and yet still has little or no effect on the core. In these situations, the potential to unlock not only incremental value but even disproportionately significant value is possible.

An example of this type of asset is your know-how and the ways of doing business that are codified in your corporate culture, traditions, and experience. Another is the technology and intellectual property your organization has developed to deliver on its business model. Amazon, the global e-retailer that developed a scalable technology to support its global business, only to realize it had also created new business-to-business services in the process, is an example of this form of edge strategy.

In the early 2000s, Amazon had started to build the complex cloud-based digital infrastructure it requires to deliver an online shopping service that operates twenty-four hours a day, seven days a week.[32] This was a costly undertaking in terms of time and money. Amazon executives realized the company was spending more than 70 percent of its time making and managing the back-end technology needed to run its business. This work was necessary to enable its core, but the functionality it provided was not uniquely useful to its business model. Its managers posited that if Amazon was investing so much in what retailers call "muck," then so too are other companies. So why not make these extensive assets available to other companies? Why not monetize this seemingly unconstrained asset?

This realization led to the formation of Amazon Web Services (AWS) in 2003. As Andy Jassy, the head of AWS, said in recent profile of the business: "One of the things we tell customers is, 'We make muck so you don't have to.'"[33] It proved a compelling sales pitch.

Today, Netflix's streaming video service comes courtesy of AWS. So does Pinterest's social network. Even the Central Intelligence Agency has placed a $600 million data storage contract with AWS, in what Jassy calls "a credibility builder."[34]

How exactly does this enterprise edge strategy work? Amazon recognized it needed to operate its core business in real time across multiple data centers. In the United States, Amazon has three huge regional computing centers—in Virginia, Oregon, and California—each with multiple buildings and thousands of servers. There are many other computing centers in countries worldwide, including Brazil, Ireland, Japan, and Singapore.[35] The company developed a key foundational asset, the web services capability, to link all these together.[36] Amazon's enterprise edge strategy was quite simply to let other companies use these web services. "In many ways, we had been working on the foundation of AWS since Amazon's inception, but didn't really know it," mused Jassy.[37]

The value proposition to Amazon's new customers was clear. Other companies "could not buy the software necessary to operate at Amazon's scale," noted Jassy. "Amazon built virtually every piece of software necessary to run a web business that could scale, on demand, to virtually any level imaginable. Only a handful of companies around the world could claim that level of software competency."[38]

Renting out this technological investment did not conflict with Amazon's core business. But it has proved an effective way to monetize the digital infrastructure, which cost billions of dollars to build.[39] Amazon CEO Jeff Bezos characterized AWS as a $5 billion business in 2015, adding that it's "still growing fast—in fact, it's accelerating."[40]

With profit margins of around 50 percent, AWS operates in a very different way from its parent company, which famously took eight years before it posted its first profit and even today sacrifices most of its margin in exchange for growth.[41] But it may yet realize the true potential of this strategy. As Jassy has boldly claimed, "AWS can be at least as big as our other businesses."[42]

Such is Amazon's belief in this enterprise edge opportunity that it is now investing more heavily in the infrastructure that supports it. By 2007, AWS was consuming more bandwidth than Amazon's websites.[43] It is, perhaps, not surprising that the *Wall Street Journal* chose to dub Jassy, "The Man Who Really Runs the Internet."[44]

––––––––––––

We will now turn to part two of this book, "Where to Unlock Value." Here we will explore in greater detail the various ways companies have used an edge mindset to advance their growth strategies or respond to market challenges. First, in chapter 5, we will return to the first form of edge strategy, the product edge, and explore the many ways companies have found to offer upselling opportunities to their customers.

PART
TWO

WHERE TO UNLOCK VALUE

CHAPTER 5

EFFECTIVE UPSELLING

Redefining "Even Better" Solutions

If you want a lesson in upselling, just drop by a local BMW dealer. If you are fortunate enough to be in its price range, there is probably a car for you. Size options of sedans are arrayed in increasing series (starting at the smallish 1 Series in some markets and escalating to the much bigger 7 Series) and as a selection of sports, SUV, and hybrid models. There are ways to vary the engine performance within a series (for example, 28, 35, 50, and M versions of the same 5 Series). But all these options simply isolate the type of car you want to buy. The upselling happens *after* you have made this selection.

We have a colleague—let's call him Tom—a BMW fan who takes pride in being a great negotiator. Tom is a bit unusual in that he quite enjoys the process of automobile shopping because, to him, getting the best price is a bit of a sport. Car dealers can suffer someone like Tom because they get volume and other back-end incentives to ease the burden of online price transparency, but the more interesting economics actually come from what Tom does to himself at the point of purchase.

Tom spends hours of research each time his three-year lease is up. An optimizer, he essentially convinces himself he has identified the best configuration for his needs and then starts a battle between dealers (over the phone) for his business. He usually wins, by his reckoning, since he is able to recapture most or all of the official spread between the published manufacturer's suggested retail price (MSRP) and the *Kelley Blue Book* wholesale price that is purportedly the dealer's only margin. Once he actually drives to the dealership to close the deal, he is in a relaxed state of mind. He has secured the prize by assuring himself he will not overpay on the big purchase (the core automobile transaction). Yet, the game is far from over.

Upon signing the papers, the dealer presents him an option to protect his new investment with a ding-resistant coating that actually makes the new car look shinier. After selecting this, he feels it would be prudent to get a wheel package in case a pothole crushes his low-profile rims (at over $1,000 replacement cost per wheel, it just seems like the right thing to do). And then, when he eventually escapes the dealership and drives away, he is upsold into a premium concierge plan from BMW Assist by the same friendly voice that initially offered to simply help "get his system set up," via satellite, over the car speakers as he drives.

All of these items are examples of upselling, presentations of product in a way that adds on to the core purchase. They are all charges that occur at or around the core purchase, but they are elected as separately priced options. Upselling doesn't necessarily sell you a better version, for a higher price. Upselling introduces a new value proposition allowing you to add on or customize once you are already psychologically committed to the base purchase. By definition, then, upselling becomes one of the most fertile grounds to apply edge strategy.

The Relationship between Pricing and Upselling

Pricing strategy is one of the fundamental instruments in a manager's toolkit. The leverage from pricing is enormous; our studies have shown that a 1 percent increase in price leads to a profit increase of more than 12 percent, on average, across the companies in the S&P index.[1] But in a competitive world, even getting small price increases is hard to do repeatedly. Customers watch the prices of your core products closely, and while every penny of a price increase drops to the bottom line, your customers need to accept it first before switching to a competitor.

The complication with pricing strategy is that it is two parts science and one part art. There is science in positioning each item you sell in the context of the strategic role it plays in your product line (for example, a signaling role, a trip-driving role, and so on). There is also science in analyzing the demand response you expect from any price changes you or your competitors make, to this or related items. Art comes with upselling techniques. These are qualitative determinations of how to price in a multipart fashion, allowing you to trade customers, step-by-step, into larger overall sales. While upselling is an art, it is far too important to be left to art alone. Looking at upselling through an edge lens gives it discipline.

Nearly every business reviews its sales per customer. The logic of focusing on this metric is that it is almost always easier to drive more revenue from those who already trust your brand and your value proposition than to acquire new customers from scratch. Sales per customer can be reviewed over different time periods, but it is commonly assessed at a transactional level as the average "ring," "ticket," "basket," or "sale." When the customer was in the moment, deliberating the purchase, did he buy everything that he wanted? Some customers might even defer all or a portion of the purchase if they can't quite complete their missions with you. Deferred purchases are bad; the customer's original impulse can go stale or, worse, she could give a competitor the chance at a later date. The goal should be to not leave the customer wanting, either by not offering her the accompanying choices she requires or by abandoning her prematurely on her journey.

Upselling, at the intersection of pricing and marketing strategy, helps round out the mission for those customers who require some ability to customize the purchase beyond the standard offer. In the business-to-business world, it might be the corporate purchaser who wants not only the product, but also a solution complete with training. In the business-to-consumer world, it might be the shopper who typically opts for the fully loaded choice. Upselling helps generate a bigger ticket by getting at more of the customer permission set. It is focused on merchandising a base product that meets the minimum requirements of the majority and then presenting separately priced options to step the relevant customers up the ladder in a way that is less arresting and more empowering than charging a higher price for the core product itself.

Effective Upselling Occurs at the Edge

The common way to capitalize on variability across customer segments is with a "good, better, best" paradigm. This approach involves developing different variants of the core product, with escalating levels of attributes, or simply increasing the number of attributes themselves. Applied to apparel, we can think of a winter jacket with greater down count, greater water resistance, more breathability and other comfort features, removable inner linings, and so on. Applied to an industrial cutting tool, it could be greater beam intensity, more precise cut calibration, increased portability, flexibility, or user-friendly features. In either case, the core product is the same, and all we have done is change the feature set and associated price for the core transaction. There is no edge strategy here; this is simply smart business.

A second way, introduced in chapter 2, involves applying the framework of outside edges. Recall that these are the most common form of edge opportunity. Unlike the prior good, better, best approach, outside edge strategies don't start out by selling differently priced variants of the core product. Rather, they involve offering the same core product to different customer segments and separately presenting upsell options. That way, customers who want an expanded offer can select into it, for a charge, at their discretion. When Starbucks tempts you with a scone to add on to your cappuccino purchase, it is capitalizing on what was originally an outside edge. These are bolt-on enhancements. They are ancillary revenue. And the purchase psychology involved is quite different, since they tend to give the customer more control over the customization process than is typically achieved selling purely premeditated variants in a single-choice transaction.

A third way, outlined in chapter 3, involves finding a journey edge and rethinking the solution so that it covers a bit more of the customer's ultimate mission (at least for those who give you permission to engage). When Home Depot upgrades your outdoor grill purchase by charging to have it "fully assembled and delivered," it is doing just this. The idea is not necessarily to sell up to a better version of the original product by adding or improving core attributes, but rather to sell up to a more complete overall solution. In this case, the bolt-on is not a feature or attribute at all, but a complementary product or service that enables or extends the value of the core offering.

As with any choice in business, there are distinct trade-offs between these options. Depending on the situation, it may be more appropriate to pursue an enhancement to the core than to offer upsell options at the edge of your product or customer journey. If your innovation is patentable or in some way protected, then incorporating it into your core offering could make a lot of sense, since the risk of having your advantage competed away is muted.

A key to edge strategy is to maintain an awareness of when an upsell is possible. We have found that if a company's focus is on its core offer and the organizational responsibilities it builds around it, management too often ignores the edge. An edge mindset is one that makes you consider both option A and option B at all times (see figure 5-1). The edge achievers identified in our study of hundreds of global companies do this consistently (see chapter 1). Taking option B can be a path to

FIGURE 5-1

Edge upselling as an alternative to core enhancement

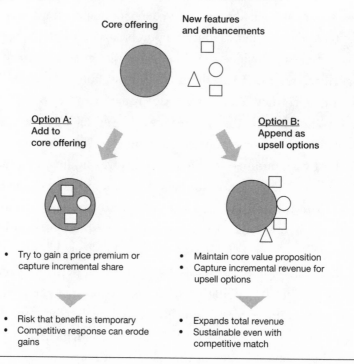

ensure that the benefits of your innovations are sustained longer than if you were exclusively focused on your core.

How to Find Add-On Options

Upselling well is not about selling harder; it is about creating the right choices. Upselling is focused on configuring features and benefits of the core offer in a way that makes it easier for different customers to recognize value. Do any of your customers feel your current offer is missing something? Some needs may be unmet because you have defined them too narrowly. In other cases, the base offer works, on average, but is not perfectly calibrated to many, or even the majority of, individual customers (who all want slightly different variants).

Sometimes you must use a combination of inside and outside product edges. An innovative solution is to reduce the core product or service to a lower common denominator and then upsell a variety of high-margin offerings to enable more personalized purchases. In general, thinking through an edge lens is great for identifying this type of opportunity. These are intuitive extensions that are tailored to customer needs that already exist in varying degrees. If merchandised correctly, upselling occurs naturally as the relevant customers select the appropriate options on their own.

Journey edges should feel equally natural. The key is catching the customer at the moment he has transacted and is immediately turning to the next step on his ultimate mission. This next step is not necessarily core, but it might not really be noncore either. If it is in a fuzzy space where you can challenge the customer permission set, you might be able to capture this next step with carefully scripted suggestive selling. It is not the equipment, but "the equipment installed and operational" that might excite the customer.

While this phenomenon is not ubiquitous, we did find evidence of it in nearly every industry we've studied. In our analysis of the world's largest corporations, we found the product edge and journey edge tactics were both prevalent upselling tools, and they were typically making among the highest contributions to overall company margins.

Product Edge Upselling

Our observations about product edge–related upsells include:

- Twenty-six percent of the companies we studied employ some form of warranty, protection plan, or extended repair and maintenance plan.

- Twenty-three percent of the companies accessorize the core purchase, and 4 percent do so in a way that deploys a discrete set of customized options (for example, from monogramming clothing to customizing military electronics).

Journey Edge Upselling

Our analysis also identified a range of journey edge–related upsells:

- Seventeen percent of companies offer to advise their customers on how to best deploy their core offering (for example, designing enterprise network systems, configuring prescription drug benefit plans).

- Fifteen percent of companies involve training, particularly in business-to-business settings.

- Eight percent of companies incorporate some form of installation-based upsell, ensuring the product is assembled, enabled, and fully functional relative to the ultimate goal the customer is trying to achieve.[2]

Two Lessons from the Best in the Business

The cruise industry has been masterful at creating opportunities to trade up. Despite a highly compelling base package, noncabin ancillaries represent about 25 percent to 30 percent of total revenue; a typical cruise passenger spends $1,304 on the actual ticket and another $415 on a range of onboard activities.[3] In studies of thousands of travelers, we have also found these add-ons tend to be simultaneously the highest margin line items and the most accretive to customer satisfaction. Patently, cruises are a bit of a special case in that once customers are on the vessel, they are captive, creating ample opportunities for cruise companies to tempt them with additional benefits. However, a deeper examination of the cruise industry provides valuable lessons for other businesses that want to improve their ability to upsell.

Founded by three Norwegian shipping companies, Royal Caribbean Cruise Lines (RCL) launched its first ship, the *Song of Norway*, with seven hundred passengers in 1970.[4] Back then, a cruise was a relatively simple concept, but the company quickly learned to add ever more all-inclusive features to attract passengers. RCL embraced a philosophy that, in cruising, the journey itself was the destination. By 1978, RCL had to cut the original *Song of Norway* vessel in two and welded in a new section to make room for more passengers and amenities.[5] In 1999, it introduced a rock-climbing wall and an ice rink on its Voyager class ships.[6] The *Allure of the Seas* now ranks alongside the biggest aircraft carriers in the US Navy fleet: it is more than a thousand feet long, weighs more than 225,000 tons, and cost Royal Caribbean more than $1 billion to build.[7] It can accommodate nearly sixty-three hundred passengers and twenty-four hundred crew members.[8] When you step onto one of its sixteen decks, you are stepping into a truly impressive floating resort; there are twenty-five different restaurants, a water park, a garden area modeled on Central Park with twelve thousand shrubs, a half-mile jogging track, an eighty-meter zip line, and a theater staging Broadway shows.[9] With all this effectively included in the base fare, how is there any opportunity to upsell the customer?

Lesson 1: Focus on the Choice before the Charge

RCL starts by selling a vacation that creates accessible luxury for a fixed base price. If you buy a ticket for a seven-day cruise around the Caribbean on the *Allure*, you can expect to pay about $800 to $900.[10] This gets you a 172-square-foot interior stateroom with a bed for two, a private bathroom, and a sitting area.[11] It also includes all-you-can-eat dining for more than eight meals per day at various restaurants, all the soft drinks you want, a range of onboard activities—from sports to shows—and access to exotic ports. Most customers don't need to go beyond this to have a truly rewarding vacation.

However, RCL also provides many choices to help those who are relaxing their minds (and wallets) indulge even further in ways that are most appropriate to them. While all passengers have access to the spa complex, higher-end spa services beckon. For gamblers, there is a big casino. Most famously, there are shore excursions. While anyone can amble off the boat into the port towns on their own, arranging a tour directly through RCL comes with the comforting assurance that the experience has been curated and preapproved, and with a guarantee that the ship won't leave without you if the tour is running late.

The key to all this is that none of those items is essential to having a great vacation. The business calculus does not start with "what else could I charge for?" but rather "where do some of my customers want to choose a different level of service?" Issuing charges for something that is required to complete a core experience is a clumsy upsell at best. But creating a differential, sometimes indulgent, higher-end choice is the subtle psychological construct that cruising has been able to tap. Every business should ask itself how it can address this natural human desire in the context of its own offer.

Lesson 2: Most Customers Really Do Want More

Even when it's "all included," most people end up wanting more. A popular misconception in upselling is that it only appeals to a minority of affluent, or perhaps irrational, customers. The truth is that, given enough degrees of freedom and the right offer calibration, most businesses can find a way to upsell most customers most of the time. The definition of "more" just varies by customer segment.

For example, RCL offers a range of seven beverage programs, focusing on premium plans that allow customers to select top-shelf liquor or wine at any time.[12] For shoppers, there is a mall, arranged over three decks, with brand-name boutiques selling jewelry, perfumes, and apparel.[13] On some Royal Caribbean ships, Park West Gallery, a specialist auction house, presents and sells art.[14] Most remarkably, even in an all-you-can-eat format, which includes lobster, steak, and midnight buffets, many foodies trade up to an even more exclusive dining experience.[15] The thing that RCL has done exceptionally well is avoid the trap of presupposing a single customer archetype. Instead, it has discerned needs that vary across customer segments and built the ability to flex its offer accordingly.

Six Types of Effective Edge-Based Upselling

If effective upselling comes down to applying product and journey edges, and identifying these edges depends on a deep understanding of customer needs, what types of needs are most common? Our research has found a pattern. In our study of six hundred major corporations, we found that the vast majority of successful upselling examples created options around one of six fundamental human needs:

1. Convenience

2. Comfort

3. Relief

4. Peace of mind

5. Passion

6. Knowledge

Type 1: Convenience Options

Convenience upselling is all about removing the hassle associated with the transaction. When you make things more convenient for your customer by helping her access or enjoy your product, you are often capitalizing on an opportunity to participate at the outside edge of your core offering. For example, when a customer rents a car from Hertz, she often doesn't want to worry about filling up the tank before returning the car, as she may be in a rush to catch a flight. Hertz recognized this need by analyzing in great detail the entire arc of each customer segment's interaction with the company and realized that it could create more convenient forms of the same service for a subset of customers who require it.

Hertz operates in 10,300 locations in approximately 145 countries around the world.[16] In the United States alone, it has a fleet of approximately 500,000 vehicles that it rents out from airports, city centers, and other convenient locations.[17] When it rents these cars and trucks, it requires customers to return them with a full tank of gas. If customers fail to do this, Hertz charges a price per gallon that is typically two or three times the price local gas stations charge.[18] This discourages customers from returning cars less than full, a phenomenon that adds both operational cost and cycle time to how quickly Hertz can turn around a vehicle for the next rental. While this may motivate the type of behavior that Hertz wants, it also creates an inconvenience for customers in a rush. Hertz has therefore devised convenient alternatives such as the Fuel Purchase Option, or FPO. With FPO, the customer can prepurchase a full tank of gas at a locally competitive price before driving the rented car off the lot.[19] This is appealing to some customers: they know that they won't have to spend valuable preflight time searching for a gas station.

As an outside edge strategy, the FPO is well designed and effective. Prepaid gas fits nicely on top of the core offering of the car rental. It also satisfies an important customer need—that of convenience and time savings. In order to activate this edge, Hertz did not need to make a major new investment, as it is delivered through the company's existing assets of sales associates and refueling infrastructure. The effort is incremental; it is refueling the cars anyway, and the upsell option is easily presented at rental initiation. Most importantly, the upsell is quite natural. A customer doesn't need the upsell to enjoy a Hertz rental, but for those who value the convenience, it is an intuitive redefinition of the offering from renting a vehicle to renting a vehicle with carefree fueling service included.

Type 2: Comfort Options

Comfort upselling means extending greater levels of ease or relaxation as customers enjoy your product. What many companies find is that two customers can enjoy the same product but desire very different degrees of pampering. A great example of this is JetBlue's "Even More Legroom" option.

A self-styled value airline, JetBlue generated $5.8 billion in revenue in 2014.[20] The company has built its brand around bringing "humanity back to air travel" and is known for its egalitarian customer service and providing a passenger experience enhanced by live television.[21] Until 2013, JetBlue offered only one class of service (that is, all coach seating).[22] This was aligned with the brand during the airline's rise in the early 2000s, but was somewhat incompatible with an edge philosophy that acknowledges customers are different and have differing demands.

Owing to a cost-cutting decision in January 2007, the layout of JetBlue's Airbus A320 fleet featured more legroom in about half the cabin. While some passengers experienced industry-leading (thirty-four inches) legroom in coach, others were randomly assigned to a roomier thirty-six-inch pitch. The differential was caused by reducing seat density so that JetBlue could fly with one fewer flight attendant (a savings of about $30 million per year at the time), but it also inadvertently created an opportunity to differentiate customers based on needs.[23]

In a moment of inspiration, JetBlue announced a branded "Even More Legroom" (EML) product in March 2008.[24] By respacing its seats yet again, a relatively simple job, the company created a comfort-based option.[25] JetBlue could now offer coach service, but also create an option to upgrade to an even roomier thirty-eight-inch pitch, which was considerably more spacious than the industry average of thirty inches.[26] "Free TVs, generous snacks, and friendly service are all part of the core JetBlue experience, and these in-flight perks will always be provided at no extra cost to the customer," said Dave Barger, then CEO of JetBlue Airways. "Our new value-added legroom product gives customers the option to make their flight even more comfortable and enjoyable."[27]

By 2011, an Even More Space product (rebranded from EML) was bringing in over $120 million in annual revenue and rising rapidly.[28] The vast majority of this incremental revenue flowed to the bottom line, because there was essentially no direct cost of providing the additional comfort to passengers. The core assets (planes and passengers) already existed. JetBlue's unique circumstances also meant it did not even need to drop the seat count to offer this feature. The seats cost $10 to $30 or more for one way, depending on the length of flight, and the option was presented à la carte, after the base fare was selected.[29] In November 2014, Jet Blue announced that it would reduce its base coach legroom to 33.1 inches and increase seat count from 150 to 165 on its A320s.[30] However, the company will continue to offer the comfort product as an edge upsell.

Type 3: Relief Options

The corollary to providing greater levels of comfort is alleviating pain points that customers experience coincident with the delivery of your product or service. This pain point may have nothing to do with anything your company is doing; it might simply be an accident of the circumstances in which you interact with your customer. However, if you can partner with your customer to relieve this annoyance, you might have an important upselling opportunity.

One of the most famous historical examples is the innovation of caller identification—or Caller ID for short. Today, when you can learn a surprising amount about the person calling you, the idea of a simple Caller ID system, which transmits a caller's number while the telephone is ringing, seems quaint. It is easy to forget how revolutionary it was when introduced. In 1987, New Jersey Bell, part of Bell Atlantic, one of seven regional telephone companies that had been spun out of AT&T three years earlier, won the right to offer a Caller ID service to residents in Atlantic City and in Hudson County, just across the river from Manhattan.[31] There were noisy opponents, who feared that this new service would be a threat to civil liberty, forcing people to reveal information about themselves that they did not want to share. Nonetheless New Jersey Bell spelled out its unique selling point. Peter Ventimiglia, a company official, told the *New York Times*: "We perceive it as the best technology available for thwarting obscene and threatening and harassing phone calls . . . It enhances the privacy of the called party. We've used the analogy of the peephole in the front door. We believe you have the right to know who's calling you before you pick up the phone."[32]

At the time, the service was clearly not an obvious part of the core telecom offering. "Call ID Service Makes Science Fiction a Reality," declared a headline in the *Los Angeles Times* in January 1990, after it was launched by New Jersey Bell. It was likened to the moment in *Back to the Future II*, a Hollywood movie released in 1989, when the character played by Michael J. Fox receives a call in 2015. On a screen, the caller's face appears, alongside his name, address, age, job title, and a list of his favorite foods.[33] It proved to be an instant hit with New Jersey Bell's customers. Asked by a *New York Times* reporter why he had subscribed to the service, which cost $6.50 per month plus a one-off payment of $60 to $80 for the special display box, Kevin Moore, a twenty-something from Jersey City, had a one-word answer: "Girls."[34] Some he wanted to hear from, others he didn't.

By 1992, some 192,000 people subscribed to the service, and other telephone companies had launched Caller ID services.[35] Bell of Pennsylvania, also part of Bell Atlantic, spent $20 million on upgrading the telephone system in Philadelphia and, in return, was expecting to generate "tens of millions of dollars" in revenues over the first five years.[36] The phone companies realized that a customer pain point was the anonymous nature of incoming calls. For a relatively modest investment, they introduced an optional add-on service to their core product of monthly phone subscription. Customers could pay a separate fee and—like magic—the name and number of the incoming caller would be revealed.

Why was this relief-oriented upsell an application of the edge mindset? The product met four key criteria. First, it leveraged the foundational assets of the telephone company: an existing subscriber base and telephone infrastructure. Second, it was delivered with incremental effort; after a relatively small capital expenditure, the phone companies only needed to flip a switch to activate the service. Third, the edge was sold for a separate financial consideration; the $5 to $10 monthly fee was incremental to the price of the core offer.[37] Fourth, the product appended naturally to the core as an option; Caller ID is useless without a corresponding phone subscription, but the base offer of the phone subscription is enhanced by the Caller ID feature.

Type 4: Peace-of-Mind Options

Peace-of-mind upselling is focused on ameliorating the anxiety that often accompanies a big-ticket purchase. Paid assurances fall into this category. Sellers of consumer electronics and white goods have long known that a customer is most susceptible to pitches for extended warrantees at the moment she is shelling out a big investment on something she could easily see malfunctioning. Our analysis across sixty-two industries of the global economy found that this type of upsell existed in 47 percent of industries; however, only 14 percent of companies within our sample have truly exploited the opportunity.[38]

One of the more salient examples is the sale of "ding protection" during the purchase of a car; the customer worries about nicks and scratches in parking lots that will lead to big charges at the end of the lease. In the example of our colleague Tom, the very act of researching and negotiating his core BMW purchase makes him vested. By the time he is signing papers, he is emotionally past the transaction and already thinking about his future interaction with the vehicle, mostly anticipated enjoyment, but also some worries. The company Dent Wizard has effectively partnered with BMW dealers and encouraged them to apply an edge-based lens to sell its protection plans at the point of sale.[39] The dealers' core business is clearly not car repair. Nor is it a risk management business. However, these services do not exactly fall outside the core either. Upselling (and earning good margin on) a ding-free experience through Dent Wizard is a natural complement that simply extends the original value proposition.

Asbury Automotive Group, a publicly traded company based in Duluth, Georgia, is among the largest sellers of cars in the United States, with dealerships carrying many brands, including BMW.[40] As we discussed in the case of our colleague Tom, customers have become savvier about shopping, using comparison websites to find the best price. Over time, this price transparency has put severe downward pressure on the profit margin that was historically realized by sellers.[41] Asbury's advantage is in being acutely attuned to the concerns of customers as they contemplate the significant purchase of an automobile. Asbury, like other dealers, recognized the opportunity to provide its customers peace of mind to relieve these anxieties. The solution was developing a system of insurance policies, assurances, protection plans, and warranties to combat every imaginable eventuality a potential car buyer fears: theft protection, crash and repair insurance, and tire-puncture coverage all fall into this bucket.

According to industry estimates, approximately 40 percent of customers who bought a new car in 2014 took out some dealer insurance—up from less than 30 percent in 2002.[42] We estimate that most dealers add about $1,000 of gross profit per vehicle from their finance and insurance (F&I) products.[43] In fact, recent industry estimates note that income from F&I products is what swings dealers from the red into the black on each new car sale; without these ancillary revenue streams, dealers would lose about $200 on each new car sold.[44] In fact, Asbury revealed that its F&I business generated 4 percent of its $5.9 billion revenues in 2014, but 23 percent of its profits. "While new vehicle sales are critical to drawing customers to our dealerships," it told its investors, "[ancillaries] generally provide significantly higher profit margins and account for the majority of our profitability."[45]

What makes this an edge strategy? The assurance plan is a material, but incremental, financial consideration on top of the original transaction. It leverages the dealership's foundational assets of the inventory-intensive car lot and steady flow of customer foot traffic; the infrastructure is already there. The incremental effort to sell the plans is relatively low. In the case of Dent Wizard products, the entire ancillary offer is outsourced, and the dealer can focus on what it does best—distributing the offering in exchange for a markup. While they remain extra charges with separate value propositions, these plans naturally complement the transaction that the dealership has already established with the customer.

Type 5: Passion Options

Passion upselling is focused on creating options that expand the experience for those customers who are the biggest fans of a brand or product. The Las Vegas show Cirque du Soleil offers insight into this approach. The circus operator, founded in Canada in 1984, aims to give superfans the opportunity to buy into an amplified version of the show that provides the special treatment that they crave.[46]

When you go to one of its touring shows—under the Big Top—or one of its resident shows in Las Vegas, Orlando, or Los Angeles, you can pay for a VIP package that gets you insider access to the show's performers. Take *The Beatles Love* show, which is staged at the Mirage in Las Vegas. As you buy a seat to the show, the company offers a trade-up option that grants direct access to the performers. If you select the premium package, you can get preferred seating, a faster entrance line, an insider access lanyard, and a one-hour backstage tour.[47] You'll see acrobats practicing, dancers rehearsing, and costume designers making last-minute repairs to some of the 331 costumes and 110 wigs used by the 68 performers.[48] "It's a perfect way to celebrate an anniversary or even impress a group or a date," say the promoters of the VIP package for *The Beatles Love* show.[49]

One of the most compelling aspects of Cirque's strategy is that it almost entirely leverages existing foundational assets. The company didn't need to build new attractions or seating; it simply gave some guests, who were willing to pay, access to what was already there. This is a classic outside edge strategy. By studying fan engagement, Cirque du Soleil realized that some circus goers wanted deeper, richer interactions with the brand. This second tier of service does not take anything away from original value proposition; it merely provides an even better offering for those who are most passionate. In our lexicon, it challenges the periphery of the customer permission set and finds that there is indeed a segment of customers who are willing to redefine, just a bit, the edge of Cirque's core offering.

A note of caution also applies. Edge plays, by definition, test the near-field opportunities that your foundational assets are largely equipped to enable. When companies step even further out into adjacent, but different spaces, the foundational asset leverage that defines the edge starts to break down quickly, and the risk profile increases. Cirque du Soleil learned this lesson firsthand. For a time, in the early 2000s, it tried to branch out, offering circus-themed hospitality and spa offerings. This was a big mistake. As Daniel Lamarre, the company's CEO, acknowledged, "Prospective partners would ask: 'What does Cirque know [about] hotels or restaurants?'"[50] The company wisely took a step back in order to focus on, as Lamarre put it, "creating incredible shows" and offering selective product enhancements for a subset of the 15 million spectators that see them every year.[51] The company regressed from a risky (and failing) move into adjacent businesses, but now drives stronger economic performance and engenders customer loyalty by focusing on the profits at its edge.

Type 6: Knowledge Options

Knowledge upselling means providing education, training, or simply situational awareness around the core offering. It is not a stretch to assume that some customers will pay for you to impart advanced know-how related to the product you are selling. When Apple sells an iMac, iPad, or iPhone, it includes some access to its Genius Bar, where customers can become acquainted with the product in a retail store through hands-on exercises with assistance and instruction.[52] These free, hour-long workshops are a cost of business for Apple since they ensure greater usage and improved loyalty from a segment of consumers who are less technically savvy. However, the company also very effectively upsells unlimited "One to One" service for $99 per year, per product.[53] By observation, many people who elect this service become less active after the first few sessions. Indeed, many never go to the sessions after purchasing the service. Accommodation of those who do is an incremental investment for Apple, though, since it tends to leverage the same staff that sells its product and provides the free clinics. Using a careful scheduling process, the company ensures it maximizes utilization of these individuals and drives to much higher margins than a third party would achieve by offering the training service.

Knowledge-based upselling is even more prevalent in the business-to-business world. For example, Nielsen N.V. is a company that is focused on providing information. The Dutch giant has over forty thousand employees, and its core offering is focused on delivering media and marketing information and analytics on what consumers are buying and watching.[54] For example, its retail measurement services estimate market share and competitive sales volumes and provide insights into the pricing and promotion activity that allows consumer-facing companies to drive their marketing and advertising strategies.[55] The knowledge-based upselling for Nielsen is clear. Initially, it began with off-the-shelf insights, but then quickly translated this into higher-margin custom research. If it is already trusted enough to provide the data that serves as the background to a marketing team's customer segmentation, it uses this basis to sell more holistic solutions to the customer. For example, it might begin with a package to provide TV usage data and then upsell online and mobile usage data, creating a much richer consumer perspective. By layering on analysis and interpretation of this data, it adds significant value for customers and greater profits for Nielsen.[56] By leveraging its relationships and the data it is selling to take one step further down the customer journey to interpretation of this data, Nielsen is exploring the fuzzy boundary of its offering by allowing some customers to buy a little more.

Our studies revealed that nearly a quarter of companies offer some knowledge-based upsell at the edge of their core product, with consulting and training being the two most common varieties.[57] In industrial sectors, it is most prevalent, with nearly 70 percent of companies offering some kind of ancillary offering through design support, certification, or other forms of supplemental advice and assistance. Nevertheless, we find the consistency of implementation is inconsistent, at best. With all the major economies becoming increasingly knowledge-based, the best practice adoption of knowledge-based options is far too varied within individual sectors, and many organizations are underexploiting this natural add-on profit stream.

Practitioner's Notes

- Edge-based upselling is distinct from the merchandising strategy of good, better, best product categorization. In upselling, you present your customers with a common core base offer and allow them to customize the purchase with optional add-ons and extras. These upsells can be built around a product or journey edge strategy.

- Using innovations and added features to enhance your core offering, bolster its competitive position, or develop good, better, best configurations runs the risk that the benefits of the strategy will be only temporary. Competitors will eventually match your upgrades and erode your gains. Instead, employing these enhancements as upsells to the core offer protects their value added, even in the face of competitive matching.

- The secret to edge-based upselling is in the calibration. Ask what your customers want that you are not providing in your current offer. If they want something slightly different from the base, determine how you can customize to exactly what they want.

- Edge-based upselling is typically customer friendly. It is merely facilitating a transaction that is needed and wanted and, in many cases, would occur anyway. The organization is doing the customer a service in the process.

- Edge-based upselling often deepens the customer relationship and builds loyalty. Try to condition customers to see your organization as their partner in choice. Promote the belief that "I, the customer, get it my way."

- Edge-based upselling is necessarily modest in its marginal commitment. It is an add-on to what you are delivering. If it's hard to deliver, you should outsource it initially to third parties better equipped to evaluate the risk, execute, and so on; you can always take over the value chain later. The power of this is partly in the fact that many small things can quickly add up.

- Much of the value in edge-based upselling is in its ease of execution. Almost certainly, some of your customers want a little bit more. These customers—and their unmet needs—are not difficult to identify. Because these opportunities are located at the edge of your business, they are not exceedingly difficult to capture.

- In summary, edge-based upselling should meet the basic criteria of edge opportunities:

  - It should leverage a set of existing foundational assets.

  - The effort (both in terms of labor and capital) to deliver the upsell should be incremental.

  - The add-on should be presented as a separate option, for separate financial consideration, that customers can use to customize their experience.

CHAPTER 6

DEALING WITH MARGIN PRESSURE
Staying Profitable Despite Headwinds

Philosophically, upselling is imbued with optimism; it implicitly assumes some customers will part with more money in exchange for additional benefits. However, edge strategies play an equally important role when the core economic model is under duress.

In most industries, the pressure on margins is both prevalent and inexorable. During average times, a large percentage of industries face significant margin deterioration. In recessionary periods, that number can skyrocket. We have observed that, within a given industry, there is often a distribution of performance in which a minority of companies are acceptably profitable, while a majority are seeking relief from cost-based stress in some material portion of their business.

Innovating to improve margins is the hallmark of true market leaders. Applying an edge mindset for combating margin pressure means recognizing that you have unprofitable customers and targeting them accordingly. Unless your core offering is highly configured for each type of customer, this means that some customers are intrinsically more valuable to you than others. In fact, some customers can actually be unprofitable and this is more common than companies often perceive.

Let us pause for a moment and reflect on this phenomenon. Unprofitable customers are an enormous burden on a business. Every time you serve or sell to them, it is dilutive. How is this acceptable?

Managing Unprofitable Customers

Inside edge strategies, in particular, can be effective at targeting unprofitable customers and helping to rectify the issues they cause. You can either cut out deadwood or directly make the problematic accounts more profitable. From an edge-oriented lens, this means identifying the parts of a core offering that customers do not universally appreciate. Once identified, you can selectively unbundle these elements so that they are no longer standard across the entire customer base. Importantly, this step does not necessitate that you reduce the base price in the newly de-contented standard offer.

Once you have made this distinction, you can charge for these marginal elements à la carte. The introduction of these options can actually create a very equitable situation. Customers who don't value these elements don't have to buy them, while those customers who do value them will now be asked to pay. Take the example of W.W. Grainger, a $10 billion distributor of maintenance, repair, and operating (MRO) supplies.[1] From safety and security supplies to lighting and electrical products, from hand tools to cleaning supplies, Grainger helps its customers get what they need to run their businesses.

Grainger builds service-level agreements with its customers around exactly what supplies it delivers where and when, and with what frequency. Nevertheless, some customers will be good and others bad, and not merely in terms of how promptly they pay their bills. Given the varied nature of their order patterns, different accounts will end up generating very different levels of profitability for Grainger. For example, rush orders, returns, and restocking activity all layer tangible cost on top of the base distribution model. Grainger can absorb a certain level of this irregular activity and could choose to go even further and tolerate outliers under the banner of good customer service. Alternatively, the company can identify which costly elements most affect its account profitability and unbundle them accordingly. In each year that a company like Grainger reevaluates variable-value elements, assessing which it should carve out and how much it should charge, results in one of three customer outcomes.

The first outcome is a protected set of accounts. This set comprises such important customers that Grainger is willing to underwrite some level of nonstandard, costly service, regardless of how much these customers value it. These customers pay for themselves, and the company needs to be careful not to antagonize them. For those who value the elements in question, Grainger creates a loyalty incentive by ascribing value to an extra level of service that they happen to enjoy for free. Grainger also explicitly demonstrates, by charging others for these elements, that customers who do not require this extra level of service are not directly subsidizing those that do.

The second outcome is a set of accounts for whom the economic equation changes. These customers now pay enough to cover the cost of providing the elements that previously made them unprofitable. Either they can pay Grainger extra for, say, restocking supplies, or they can modify their behavior to demand less of this costly activity. This group now produces an acceptable margin, but only because of the inside edge strategy that required them to pay more. This clearly changes the deal for them, and you must handle communication carefully. The important thing to remember is that inside edges do not result in the imposition of mandatory fees. Instead, they create a distinction between a basic option that is clearly acceptable to many, and voluntary options that can be used to build a fuller-service solution. The fact that you must charge for variable-value elements that were previously given away makes this the most awkward of all edge strategies to implement. Nevertheless, this change is justified when it provides a more sustainable economic situation.

The third outcome is a set of customers who were previously unprofitable and now choose to defect rather than pay a new à la carte charge tied to the variable-value element. The fact that they leave may be painful to watch, but it can ultimately be a very good thing. Imagine that one of Grainger's customers demanded expedited shipping four days per week, driving significant real cost and opportunity cost. Unbundling expedited shipping and charging for unplanned truck rolls would be an appropriate response. That way Grainger could be fairly compensated for the nonstandard burden of servicing the customer at that level. If that customer chose to walk away instead of paying for the extra level of service, we don't suppose that Grainger would mind. In the same way that you would shut down an unprofitable factory, close unprofitable stores, or terminate an unprofitable product line, so too should you aim to reduce the number of unprofitable customers you serve.

In our study of the world's largest companies, we found that 8 percent employed an inside edge strategy of this sort.[2] The impetus for de-contenting or unbundling the offer is nearly always margin compression. But this is really a mechanism to segment customers based on profitability. We have also found evidence of this strategy, most prevalent in financial services, in sectors of the economy as diverse as industrials, consumer staples, and health care.[3] In the pages that follow, we profile how the US airline industry used this strategy to fundamentally transform its economic position.

How the US Airline Industry Found Its Edge

Ever since Leonardo da Vinci started sketching designs for flying machines in his notebook, aviation has attracted bold, blue-sky thinking. But since deregulation in 1978, airlines in the United States have done everything Da Vinci could have asked of them, except make money.[4] Between 2001 and the end of 2008, for example, no fewer than fifteen US airlines filed for bankruptcy.[5] Around 2008, however, something unexpected occurred. Airline performance suddenly leveled off. In the past few years, profits have become positive across the industry, and market capitalizations are soaring from prior lows.[6]

So what happened? The turnaround can't be attributed to a bold initiative such as new carbon-fiber aircraft, the pioneering of new markets, or even low-cost innovation. Rather, it was the result of something far more modest: the slicing of airlines' base offerings into customizable options and extras. For many airlines, this simple innovation was the difference between survival and insolvency. For us, it provides the quintessential example of an inside edge strategy applied to combat margin challenges.

Toward the end of 2007, John Tague, a rising executive and future president of United Airlines, the third-biggest carrier in the United States, held a series of meetings with his leadership team at the company's sprawling Elk Grove campus near Chicago. For much of the previous five years, Tague and his team had battled to get United Airlines out of bankruptcy and back into profitability.[7] By 2006, they had achieved this goal, but their work was far from complete. In fact, by our estimates, the vast majority of airlines worldwide had failed for years to return their cost of capital to investors. And against this sick-industry backdrop, United, Delta, and American Airlines were among the lowest of the low on the basis of economic profit (operating income adjusted for a capital charge) of a total of eighty global airlines that we analyzed.[8]

The price of oil had started to spike upward. In January 2007, Brent crude was $54.30 per barrel, but by the end of the year, it had risen to $91.45.[9] Fuel was already a significant cost for the airlines, accounting for around 25 percent of United's operating expenses at the time.[10] So a doubling of the oil price could have been catastrophic. Also, in the wake of the financial crisis and the onset of the Great Recession, businesses slashed travel budgets, and the cost-conscious leisure segment opted to travel less. The word "staycation"—spending your holiday at home—joined the common parlance. In 2007, United's passenger revenue was $15.3 billion, but had commenced a two-year, 22 percent downward march.[11] The airline was shrinking as quickly as it could to right-size its capacity to a "new normal" level of market demand, but margins were not only declining; they had turned negative again.[12]

Having recently emerged from bankruptcy and unable to maintain strong economic performance in a dog-eat-dog industry plagued with low barriers to market entry, extraordinary capital costs, and margin-eroding price transparency, United had to determine how to keep flying profitably. To combat an untenable situation, Tague and his team devised a series of what we would term edge strategies. Central to this thinking was challenging the inside edge of the offer and creating options designed to turn unprofitable customers into profitable ones. With the pressure for action at an all-time high, Tague decided to accelerate the introduction of a particular change that he knew would be the most controversial: the now-notorious checked bag fee.

In those days, a typical airfare covered the cost of traveling from point A to point B. It also allowed passengers to take up to two bags per trip. The cost of supporting this is significant; from the moment you check your bag, it is tagged, scanned, and sent via conveyer belt to be handled, sorted, and loaded into the belly of a plane, often with little elapsed time before takeoff. At the other end of the flight, much of the process is reversed before you collect your belongings at baggage claim. The multiple airline employees who touch the bag cost money. The IT systems, conveyers, and vehicles must also be operated and maintained. A customer service staff is employed to clean up after inevitable logistical service failures. Finally, there is the incremental cost of jet fuel for each checked bag, the weight (up to fifty pounds) of which must be carried into the air two to four times per round-trip ticket (depending on connections).

The logic of applying an inside edge framework here is self-evident. The cost of United's defined service provision exceeded the average revenue it could collect, forcing it to revisit the very definition of its core offering. An obvious place to look, in retrospect, was a segmentation of customers based on how lightly they pack. Bags cost money, but not everyone needed bag-check services. For example, the highest-yielding passengers, business travelers, often didn't check bags at all. Yet in a one-size-fits-all model, those who didn't want this service effectively subsidized those who did. So, in February 2008, one month before the oil price broke through the $100-per-barrel barrier, United announced that passengers could continue to check one bag for free, but if they wanted to check a second bag, they would be charged a $25 fee.[13]

United took great care when implementing the strategy to protect its more valuable customers. Basically, if you were a profitable customer for United, almost nothing changed for you. Those who gave the company consistent business were likely already "elites" in United's Mileage Plus loyalty program, and they were exempt from any charges.[14]

Most importantly, business is business. Margin pressure forced United to make some hard choices, and it demonstrated that it was willing to make a conscious trade of some consumer backlash in exchange for a rational and, arguably, more equitable structure. Parsing out the inside edge of the business proved a more strategic way to square the circle of profitability than many slash-and-burn alternatives. At their heart, edge strategies deal with different customers differently.

While much is credited to industry consolidation, ancillary revenue remains the difference between profit and loss for the airlines. Nearly all the major airlines quickly followed United's lead and went on to differentially price for both first and second bags.[15] While many consumers decried the loss of their windfall, it is questionable whether it has actually hurt the airlines much. One airline, Delta, actively managed perception with a marketing campaign focused on how it was reinvesting billions into the customer in the form of value-added capital projects and, ultimately, a better product.[16] According to J.D. Power and Associates, a researcher of consumer satisfaction, Delta now has better customer feedback than it did before the institution of bag fees.[17]

Then there are the economic results. In 2014, according to the US Bureau of Transportation Statistics, US airlines earned $3.5 billion in baggage fees. Between 2012 and 2014, ancillary revenues averaged approximately 2 percent of total operating revenue, but delivered an astonishing 37 percent of industrywide operating income.[18]

A Platform for Further Innovation

This edge mindset also paved the way for many outside edge innovations. The more recent evolution of this optionality has focused on the techniques we described in chapter 5—upselling passengers to an improved experience. Application of the outside edge mindset has led to selling fast-track boarding, lounge access, extra legroom, and premium food and beverage choices. In 2014, the major US airlines earned an estimated $15.4 billion from such "ancillary revenue" alone, grown from a negligible base eight years prior.[19] Since the capability to provide these services was often already in place, all the airlines had to do was provide passengers with an ability to buy them.

Characteristic of the edge strategies we have outlined, these relatively incremental efforts proved highly profitable. United, along with some of its rivals, has seen its fortunes rise dramatically. From 2003 to 2007, when they were digging themselves out of bankruptcy, United and Delta sat at the foot of our economic profit performance table (see table 6-1). By contrast, from 2009 to 2014, both United and Delta ranked at the top of the table, ahead of Emirates, Southwest, and more than seventy other airlines that previously outranked them.[20]

Breaking the Service Bundle

In chapter 5, we discussed how services could be layered onto a core offering to create an upsell opportunity, charging more and delivering more only to those who value the added-on elements. Yet what if the services are already included in the standard offering but, again, not universally valued?

As in the prior discussion, we are still solving an optimization equation in a world where the end goal is more profitable customers. However, while one application of the edge mindset is manifested in pricing strategy (charge more for doing more), another approach is to

TABLE 6-1

Airline profit performance

Rank (2010–2014)	Company	2005–2009 Economic profit	2010–2014 Economic profit	Ranking: 2010–2014 versus 2005–2009
1	Delta Air Lines / Northwest Airlines	($5,824 million)	$9,660 million	⬆⬆ 76
2	United Airlines / Continental Airlines	($4,168 million)	$6,957 million	⬆⬆ 72
3	U.S. Airways / American Airlines	($5,210 million)	$6,725 million	⬆⬆ 73
4	Japan Airlines	($5,995 million)	$3,708 million	⬆⬆ 74
5	Emirates	$910 million	$3,527 million	⬇ (4)

Source: L.E.K. analysis.

Note: Economic profit defined as shareholder returns in excess of cost of capital.

simply reduce the product or service cost to create an economic surplus (charge less, but do less). This involves pulling the cost lever (as opposed to the revenue lever). As in upselling, a mismatch of your core offering exists with the customer permission set for at least a subset of customers. Like upselling, you also start by redefining—and therefore redesigning—your core offering to address this asymmetry. But in this case, you engineer a smaller or de-contented offering. Stripping away services at the edge of your product or journey and making them separately salable allows more precise calibration to different customer segments. In this way, self-service is an inside edge response to margin pressure.

For example, take the case of gasoline stations. While self-service gasoline is a market standard in the United States today, this was not always the case. The original core offering included an attendant to not only pump your gas, but also wash your windshields, check your oil, and then take payment.[21] Going back in history to when this inside edge strategy was deployed provides interesting insight into the motivations and execution of a now intuitive de-contenting strategy, one that ultimately proved highly customer-friendly.

Using Self-Service to Increase Margins

Pumping gasoline is a very low-margin business. For every gallon of fuel, a gas station makes a profit of just three cents, equating to a profit margin of 1 percent or less. However, 80 percent of gas in the United States is distributed via gas stations with convenience stores. While these stations still generate more than two-thirds of their top line revenue from gas sales, two-thirds of their profit is derived in other ways, such as selling snacks, coffee, and other items to the people buying the gas. It's not surprising that over the years, they have worked to innovate and evolve the core model.[22] The initial shift took place by redefining the edge of this core service with the arrival of self-service pumps. The story begins in 1947 at Frank Urich's convenience store in Los Angeles.[23]

A born entrepreneur, Urich opened the world's first self-service gas station. This was long before automation, so he still required some attendants, typically gliding from pump to pump on roller skates collecting cash and resetting the meters for the next customer.[24] But the reduction in labor costs was significant and meant that Urich could offer his customers a better deal.[25]

Yet, for all this, the gas stations that offered full service continued to dominate the business.[26] It helped that these were mostly owned by deep-pocketed oil companies that spent a fortune lobbying state regulators to prohibit their self-service rivals.[27] Two years after Urich's pioneering move, New Jersey was persuaded to prohibit self-service gas stations. They are still banned there.[28]

Despite technological improvements, skepticism about self-service continued to reign. In 1966, two years after the introduction of automated pumps, there were still just seventeen states that permitted self-service gas stations.[29] Also, many proprietors did not think customers would accept a reduced service.[30] Why would they want to get out of the car to fill up the tank when there was someone ready and willing to do it for them?

Then came the tipping point for the industry. In March 1974, when the OPEC oil embargo was lifted, oil prices had quadrupled to $12 per barrel.[31] Contrary to popular perception, gas stations do not do well when the price of gas rises quickly. A highly competitive industry, gas stations are forced to reduce their markup when their wholesale cost increases, leading to a lag before wholesale price increases translate to retail prices, putting margins under severe pressure. Moreover, the shock itself resulted in an elastic response from economically strapped consumers.[32]

Margin compression forced gas stations to revisit the successive self-service edge strategies they had tried in the past. The solution to flagging industry profits could be solved by fractionating the cost of serving different customer groups, depending on their varying need for the service element that had long accompanied fueling. The tide shifted. By 1982, some 72 percent of all gas sales came from self-service stations, up from just 16 percent in 1969.[33]

Importantly, the innovation required a relatively minimal investment in the new technology. Imagine you own a station. The location is already selected on a well-trafficked route, the regulated underground tanks are already approved, and the convenience store is already in place. In this case, the incremental dollars to create an automated option would be relatively modest, but it would enable a very different cost structure. Interestingly, this example is a case where the stripped service model proved even more popular than the fully loaded original. Self-service now accounts for about 90 percent of US gas sales. Unpacking services from what was previously bundled creates a customer choice that is a true win-win. The self-service model lowers the cost to the consumer by approximately 10 percent.[34] For the operating stations, it simultaneously results in a doubling of daily gasoline profit.[35]

As we observe increasing efforts to bring self-service checkout to the worlds of grocery stores, home improvement stores, and other retail settings, we are witnessing not only the march of technology but analogous applications of the same phenomenon we saw in gas stations. In an overbuilt, declining comparable-store-sales environment, retailers of all sorts also face severe pressure on already razor-thin margins. By unpacking their own service bundles, they are challenging the inside edge of what it means to be a retail distributor. Transacting doesn't necessarily require a human touch, and if technology can reduce labor cost and, in some cases, increase customer satisfaction through expedited checkout, then what is now sporadically offered as a choice may soon also become the predominant market standard.

Using Self-Service to Preserve Margins

What is the fundamental cause of margin pressure? Typically, it is a function of one or both of two forces working against your organization. In the first instance, cost creep has imposed itself upon your corporate fabric, meaning that the increasing complexity of delivering your core offer, often as a result of growth, no longer adheres to the original business model. The second cause is increased competitive rivalry; others have sufficiently mimicked your offer such that the balance of pricing power has shifted out of your favor and back to the customer. In either case, it is unsustainable to continue along the current path.

As we have tried to underscore, any edge-based solution to this problem must begin by analyzing your offer through the eyes of your customer. The medical device world provides a fascinating example of companies doing just that. By deeply investigating the components of their offer from a customer perspective, some of these organizations are challenging their product and journey edges to combat forces threatening to erode their profitability.

Take, for example, Smith & Nephew, one of the leading manufacturers of knee and hip implants. The company is one of five major players that collectively control 95 percent of the US hip and knee replacement market.[36] Sales reps at device makers like Smith & Nephew have traditionally had a major presence in the operating room—helping surgeons select the appropriate tools for procedures. This is an important role. Sales reps consult with the doctors immediately prior to an operation, bringing multiple implants and advising what devices might work best. It is not uncommon for the rep to help doctors navigate more than a dozen product trays in a single surgery, each with hundreds of instruments.[37]

Health-care reform has created margin pressure on the hospitals that are Smith & Nephew's clients. Declining reimbursement rates, lower-cost procedures, and payor pressure have all contributed to significantly increased cost-savings targets, and they have started to look carefully at their partners. The high-value sales rep support that Smith & Nephew provides these hospitals is extremely costly; it generally accounts for 40 percent of the final price of an implant.[38] Hospitals have noted this and have started to push back.

Smith & Nephew could have responded in the form of pure discounting, compromising its margins and inviting competitors into a devastating price war. Worse, once price is lowered for some hospitals, it would become exceptionally hard to hold it for others. However, by revisiting the scope of its core offer, Smith & Nephew discovered an inside edge that it could parse out. Not every hospital valued the sales rep service equally. Some found the service less valuable, as they had developed in-house capability to assist surgeons with tool selection. Some had also started to become wary of having suppliers so close to clinical decisions. Others had merely started to bristle at paying for bundled selling. Whatever the reason, there was clearly an opportunity to pioneer a model where, in exchange for a reduced price, sales reps no longer provided technical support to operating room staff.

Smith & Nephew's "rep-less" program is called Syncera. When announcing the new sales model during a July 2014 investor call, the company estimated that its hip and knee products would be sold for a 30 percent to 40 percent discount through the program and that 10 percent of its customers would participate in the new model. Syncera offers only past-generation products and does not include direct sales rep support. This version of the product will use an iPad app, instead of human hand-holding, to help surgeons navigate tool selection.[39]

The paradigm shift is spreading across the industry; numerous surgical device companies seem to either be considering or outright embracing it.[40] The approach is not expected to cannibalize mainline sales and is aimed squarely at preserving margins. "We feel the model can coexist with the traditional model," said Stuart Morris-Hipkins, general manager of the Syncera business for Smith & Nephew.[41]

Like many edge strategies that require reconditioning customers around new product definitions, it is accretive at the industry level and improved by wider competitive adoption. The rep-less model has reduced costs for both the suppliers and their hospital customers.[42]

At the time of writing, this shift is very new. The jury is out on whether this will stick permanently or will alone be enough to stem the tide of margin pressure for implant suppliers. Regardless, it is a highly innovative approach. It applies a classic inside edge mindset to the core offer and effectively creates options that heretofore did not exist. Other manufacturers have introduced different inside edge strategies aimed at reducing their footprint (for example, remote teleconference, drop shipping, direct shipping). We believe we are seeing the beginning of an exciting wave of strategic moves applied in an effort to, as our health-care partners say, "bend the cost curve."[43]

Vignette: A Nonprofit Application in Cash-Strapped Schools

An unfortunate consequence of the Great Recession is that many US municipalities face severe budget pressure. Tax revenue decreased, state funding was curtailed, and massive cuts in school funding resulted. This shortfall existed in the context of ever-rising school expenses. By some estimates, the average cost of educating a student had skyrocketed by over 40 percent in the two decades preceding the crisis.[44] This is the public-sector equivalent of margin compression or, more precisely, of operating deeply in the red.

Many school districts reconciled this by simply cutting whole departments (music and foreign languages were typical candidates) or by deleting entire sports and extracurricular programs.[45] By contrast, other schools addressed the issue in a different way, by finding and isolating the inside edge of the core educational offer. The strategy on the part of these latter educators was to challenge the one-size-fits-all model, reduce the level of foundational content, and then allow those who most value the newly classified elective services to buy back in. "Students have to realize, as our country is realizing, that you can't have everything," said Randy Stepp, superintendent of schools in Medina, Ohio. "We all have to make tough choices."[46]

Given that different student segments have intrinsically different needs, this sounds like an inside edge approach to us. The interesting thing about these elective charges is that they are, by definition, optional. Students are not charged for English or math. In some cases, the incremental cost to the "customer" is zero. If your child never had any intention of taking French or running track, then nothing has changed for you. However, if a parent views these as essential to a child's upbringing or college-prep plan, she still has an option to buy back in to the more robust suite of offerings that was previously available. While this à la carte model has proved controversial, we would argue this is a far better solution for everyone than an alternative that many districts have taken to simply reduce the scope of education for all.[47]

The point here is not that everyone is better off; life is filled with challenges for which there is no quick fix. But applying an edge mindset can create an equitable construct to accommodate needed cost reduction, where less of what matters is lost by fewer people. In the words of Collene Van Noord, superintendent of schools in Palmyra, Pennsylvania, "If we can pass on the added costs for some of our more expensive courses to direct users, it seems more fair than to pass them on to the entire community [in the form of tax hikes]."[48]

Practitioner's Notes

- The trouble with many core offerings is that you are, in effect, giving away parts of your products and services for free to those who don't value them. You can be left with some unprofitable customers, which is certainly undesirable and may be unsustainable in the long term. As we saw with upselling opportunities, margin compression often forces us to view and ultimately treat customer segments differently.

- Inside edge strategies, in particular, are promising mechanisms for combating margin pressure. Fundamentally, this is a calibration exercise.

  - If a significant number of customers demand features and attributes that are less than the standard offer, then the edge of the product can often be better mapped to a new de-contented state.

  - At that point, the company can either capture the surplus and charge more (fees) of those who want more than the new standard or do less to reduce the overall cost of service.

- In the case of "do less" inside edge opportunities, the organization can either capture all of the cost savings for itself or share some of the newly found economic surplus directly with the customer in a win-win proposition. In situations where the organization keeps the surplus, it can still share benefits with the customer indirectly via increased investment in improving the core offer.

- Finding the inside edge often starts by challenging whether each of the features and attributes that are part of the core product is really equally valued by everyone.

  - Features that are not universally valued (and exceed the redefined minimum) are candidates for strategies that involve product redefinition.

- Customers that only value the true minimum typically experience no change with the introduction of a de-contented product or service.

- Other customers, who are intrinsically less profitable, must support the incremental cost they are driving by buying back into the fully loaded offer.

- Customers who are already highly profitable should be treated separately and not charged for the decoupled features.

• In a world of constrained resources, edge strategy creates constructive choices that allow more people to ultimately get what they want. Even if some people are a bit worse off economically, they are better off having a choice of whether to experience less of the offer or to buy back in; the alternative is a blanket judgment that leaves many people categorically worse off.

CHAPTER 7

BEATING THE COMMODITIZATION CYCLE

Sharpening Differentiation with Less Risk

Rise-and-fall is a repeated pattern; the fleeting nature of competitive advantage stems from a tendency of all products to commoditize over time. Competitors are forever encroaching, replicating advances, and muting differentiation. As soon as customers are presented with acceptable alternatives, they tend to fixate on price and challenge profitability. The problem is aggravated as technology makes copying product features easier, faster, and cheaper. The only way to restore advantage is to evolve, but even innovation seems impotent when it subsidizes competitors' R&D.

While there is no sustainable way to prevent this commoditization cycle, edge strategy is often the best weapon to combat its effects. In the last chapter, we discussed how inside edges could be used to deal with the type of margin pressure that results from cost creep. In this chapter, we will examine how to apply a combination of product edges and journey edges to the type of margin pressure that results from excess competition.

Some of the most effective underlying marketing techniques to combat commoditization are not new; they include customization, solution selling, and, in certain cases, bundling. This particular triumvirate is both hard and expensive to execute. However, we argue that applying an edge mindset to approximate these techniques leads to strategic moves that are easier, cheaper, and highly effective. Reframed, these three strategic moves are:

1. Edge-based customization

2. Edge-based solutions

3. Edge-based bundling

The first move, edge-based customization, uses ancillaries as a faster, less capital-intensive way to support product configuration. The second, edge-based solutions, dissuades customers from price shopping by using edges to amplify the value of products or services. The third, edge-based bundling, demonstrates how wrapping edge offerings around core offerings can create meaningful differentiation when many options exist.

When used in conjunction, these three strategic moves collectively create a dynamic merchandising approach that both improves customers' experience and broadens their perception of value. The repeated, successive application of these three strategic moves helps organizations get closer to customers, defend against commoditization, and, over the long run, preserve margins.

Let's begin with how product edges can enable virtual customization—in other words, how you can apply the same strategies described in chapters 5 and 6 to provide some of the benefits of customization without the burdens of actually going all the way down an otherwise challenging path.

Edge-Based Customization

Customization is the ultimate weapon against commoditization. If you can truly convince customers that the product they are buying is unique to them and built for them, then it becomes quite hard to compare it to a competitive equivalent. The ultimate form of this core strategy is bespoke, or custom-made. Literally, a product is produced from raw materials to the customer's exact specification; it is a one-of-a-kind. There is no prefabrication in this model; the manufacturing or production process occurs entirely after the order is secured. The immediate example of this is high-end tailoring: a customer has detailed measurements taken, and skilled tailors literally cut cloth from spools of fabric and sew them together to make a piece of clothing to the customer's exact measurements.

There are many other examples; having a custom home built takes on a similar model, as does a major engineering project such as commissioning the construction of a new ship. In these cases, the customer specifies in advance everything he wants to see in the product and the supplier builds to that specification. In our circle diagrams in chapter 2, these would represent a perfect eclipse situation. The customer permission set is fully met, since the offer has been built specifically to do so. The trouble with this model is that you cannot use any scale efficiencies, and you need to have a highly skilled workforce to execute such customized production efforts.

If you have ever explored tailored clothing providers, you might have discovered offerings of made-to-measure custom clothing. This apparel is marketed to offer you a more personalized product at much more affordable prices than it would cost for true bespoke.[1] These companies rarely make your product from scratch, but rather have a broad range of templates. While they take measurements as a bespoke tailor does, their production solution is a modular one. Essentially, they configure your product using a range of predetermined elements. The product you buy is indeed relatively made-to-order and has been configured to feel sartorial enough to satisfy all but the most discerning customers. They can offer it to you at a lower price because there are indeed some economies of scale, and this model requires less specialized labor than truly personalized tailoring. Similar modular solutions exist in home building and industrial products. In all cases, the companies are trying to use customization to avoid price comparison and the threat of commoditization.

In much the same way, *edge-based customization* can be a faster and easier way to offer customization. It involves the active use of edge strategy to enable product configuration without having to make fundamental changes to how you produce your core offering. Identifying product edges to your core provides the building blocks so that a customer can customize his own offering along prioritized dimensions.

Hotels are an interesting example of a service industry that is finding new ways to execute exactly this strategic move. Some hotel companies have realized that they must pursue a more sophisticated segmentation of guest needs and compete in a more "customized" way to prevent commoditization of their offerings. Today they are starting to use edge-based customization to compete.

At a high level, there are four sets of actors in the hotel business: property owners, management companies, distribution partners, and the hotel brands themselves. Since many of the big hotel companies have gone "asset light" over the last couple of decades, the property owners are typically real estate investment trusts, wealthy individuals, or family funds.[2] The owners are focused on identifying underserved locations, selecting valuable real estate, building attractive facilities, and striking deals with the other three actors. The management companies and distribution partners play important roles, but are largely middlemen taking direction, and fees, from either the property owners or the hotel brands. The hotel brands are the drivers of product innovation; they are focused on defining and managing brand standards, devising marketing messages, and improving the systems (computer reservations, loyalty programs, and so on) that pump customers into their networks.

The traditional way to make money in the hotel industry has been to bet successfully on the right property, ensure consistent service delivery, and then ruthlessly manage costs to disciplined standards, while not overpaying for distribution. This formula ensures that a hotel is on the right side of the supply-demand equation through a full economic cycle. Thus, there has historically been little tolerance for anything that adds operational complexity, such as nonstandard guest options. Most hotels still offer scant choices for customers: defined check-in and checkout times, limited room selection, and some very basic extras, such as a minibar and on-demand movies.

Commoditization remains a continuous threat in the hotel industry as well. Online travel agencies are a double-edged sword for hotels. While they provide valuable customer flow, they also charge commissions of 15 percent to 20 percent and simultaneously facilitate margin-damaging price discovery.[3] Moreover, they compete, with their own loyalty programs, to be customers' first point of call for every time they stay. Commoditization pressures are only exacerbated by the fact that hotels have traditionally classified themselves by price tier (for example, luxury, upscale, midscale, budget, and so on), allowing for quick comparisons across highly comparable star-rating alternatives in popular locations.

However, hotels have started to fight back. The big hotel companies are all racing to develop lifestyle brands that resonate with customers on the basis of personality versus the traditional metrics of location, star rating, room size, and price.[4] But building or buying new hotel brands is an expensive business. It takes ages to execute. It also doesn't solve the original problem with the thousands of hotels that are already victims of commoditization pressure. For the bulk of the business, edge strategy can provide a simpler, higher ROI alternative.

Armed with a trove of data, some hotel luxury brands have begun to create options for their customers. These options are classic outside product edges. They are not new adjacent offerings, but rather enhancements that lie just on the outer rim of what could be considered the core hotel offering. Examples include reaching out to customers who were known golfers to prebook tee times, helping known foodies schedule reservations at in-house restaurants and spas, or selectively upselling to better rooms or suites prior to arrival. While many of these options existed in some form or fashion, most hotels had not explicitly parsed out and presented them in this way before. The edge strategy is clearly to allow the core transaction to happen naturally and then be proactive about merchandising selective outside product edges as separate add-on enhancements.

This approach is transforming a relatively competitive product, a luxury hotel room, into a more customized experience. The enablers of this strategy were intrinsically present; the existing hotel facilities, flow of guests, and communication channels were all existing foundational assets that could be leveraged. The success of this strategy does not require new customers. Nor does this approach create truly new adjacent services. It simply uses edge-based customization to redraw the boundaries around the core offering in a way that makes it easier for guests to recognize and select into additional value. An edge strategy such as this is fabulously less expensive than other types of hotel innovation, such as building and branding new concepts.

What we have described is a migration from a relatively standard core product to a more malleable, customizable construct. Sometimes, this begins with selective unbundling of features to create more flexibility. Always, it involves creating enhancements that can be upsold to deliver a near-unique solution. But the inside and outside edges that enable edge-based customization are only the first move in defending against commoditization. The next move involves identifying journey edges that are used to turn a product transaction mentality into the deeper customer connections that are made by providing solutions.

Edge-Based Solutions

Most decommoditization efforts begin and end with the construction of solutions. Solutions redirect customers from haggling over the prices of features and benefits and instead focus them on completed outcomes. As we will see, edge-based solutions are often the easiest and least risky way to enact this strategy.

A salient example of where edge-based solutions are already being put in practice today is the industrial gas industry. Air Products & Chemicals (Air Products) provides a great illustration of how to use journey edges to migrate customers from product decisions to broader mission decisions and, in the process, remove some of the transactional mentality that leads to commoditization.

Air Products is a more than $10 billion supplier of industrial gases, performance materials, equipment, and technology. It is the world's largest provider of hydrogen and helium and has leading global supply positions in markets such as semiconductor materials, refinery hydrogen, coal gasification, natural gas liquefaction, and advanced coatings and adhesives.[5] While scale represents a significant barrier to entry in this business, various players compete in the space, and hydrogen and helium, as basic elements, are prone to commoditization pressures.

To defend against these pressures, Air Products has become an adept edge-based solution marketer. The company carefully wraps services, which all fit our definition of journey edge offerings, around its core business of gas supply to the air separation facilities. This allows Air Products to move away from marketing the underlying gases and instead focus on complete solutions. For example, the high-purity gases such as nitrogen, oxygen, and argon that are used in semiconductor fabrication require input from Air Products.[6] If a semiconductor customer made its decision strictly on the best price for the commodity elements that it needs for its distillation, Air Products would be unlikely to eke out an acceptable margin. However, the company not only offers a variety of optional services but positions them alongside the gas supply as broader solutions. For example, it offers, among other services:

- Plant assessment services that evaluate customer facilities and help to increase production, efficiency of power consumption, safety, and reliability.

- Operations and maintenance services that staff customers' plants with experienced personnel to assist with ongoing requirements.

- Spare parts and inventory control to ensure that mission-critical repairs are managed from a single source.

- Advisory services on operating at peak efficiency and availability by leveraging Air Products's experience across hundreds of comparable industrial gas plants.

- Safety training on how to best handle and work with the gases and related equipment within customers' facilities.[7]

Selling solutions is a well-understood theme. Solutions essentially help companies sell more core products by explicitly calling out a broader need, augmenting appropriately, and giving it a meaningful wrapper. What makes edge-based solutions so attractive is that the highest-leverage applications tend to be at the edge of the customer journey. It is the first place to look to assist with more of the customer's mission in a way that is both natural and credible.

In the case of Air Products, the supply chain is already established, and technical engineers are routinely onsite at their customers' operations. Any service that walks another step on the journey to how the gases are ultimately being used helps transform a flow of transactions into a true partnership. In this manner, Air Products people and capabilities become virtual extensions of their customers' own staff.

Armed with edge-based customization and an edge-based solutions framework, you have the building blocks needed to start reconstructing newly calibrated offers. These are not wholesale changes to the core business, but rather a gentle redefinition around the edges to present different versions of the offer that are more holistic, easily recognizable, and highly attractive solutions for different customers.

Edge-Based Bundling

Bundling is a process by which you roll together products or product features into a single offering. Bundling makes buying easier, but it can also reduce customers' ability to directly benchmark prices on

core products. It also underpins the third key application of edge strategy to help preserve margins in the face of commoditization threats.
Specifically, *edge-based bundling* is the process by which edge options
that either have been carved out of the original offer and/or have been
augmented are proactively reassembled in a way that resonates more
strongly with distinct customer segments.

Bundling is not always required; in fact, sometimes it is a suboptimal
marketing strategy, for example, when you are upselling with a limited
number of options. However, when edge-based customization multi-
plies the number of options, edge-based bundling can help simplify the
sale and expand the pie. Edge-based bundling recognizes that customers do not immediately see the benefits of edge-based customization
and solutions. It targets very specific customer segments in ways that
are relevant to them.

The aim of this third strategic move goes beyond aggregating
attributes that hang well together and, more pointedly, focuses on
cleverly combining edge and core offerings to build powerful differentiation. Perfectly executed, edge-based bundling should not only
facilitate the sale but also enhance the overall value proposition. The
components used in edge-based bundling are not merely additive, but
synergistic.

The story of the US telecom industry, introduced in chapter 5, demonstrates how an outside product edge, Caller ID, was used to *enhance
margins* through effective upselling. Where the telecom companies
went next provides an intuitive illustration of how further development
of edge strategy can also *preserve margins* in the face of commoditization trends.

For roughly a century after Alexander Graham Bell received the
first telephone patent in 1876, the revenue model in telecommunica-
tions centered on minutes of access (that is, how long you talked on the
phone). Over time, different rate cards were developed that split phone
charges into local, long-distance, and international calling. Also, the
associated cost-per-minute billing often reflected bandwidth demands
that increased during busier times of the day or week. However, in the
latter part of the twentieth century, technology marched on, allowing

a host of edge products to proliferate on largely similar technical infrastructure.

Caller ID was certainly not the only enhancement introduced. Telecoms enabled other value-added services such as the ability to convey messages in absentia through voice-mail boxes and the ability to field and toggle inbound calls through call-waiting.[8] None of these was fundamentally the core service. Nor were any of these really adjacent businesses. They were optional ancillaries that enhanced the core offering for those who valued these specific features.

As we discussed earlier, each of these edge-based options leveraged the foundational assets of the telecom provider in a powerful way. Only incremental investment was required to present options that paired with the core access model. First, the enhancements tended to generate the highest gross margins of any service offering (since the core access model already bore so much of the cost to enable them). Second, the pairing encouraged customers to view the offering as more of a differentiated solution. No longer were quality of service (which quickly converged on an acceptable standard) and price (which was easily comparable across competitive rate cards) the only meaningful attributes.

Value-added services allowed customers to construct a suite of products that addressed a broader mission: communication on their own terms. Additionally, some of these new services had a learning curve that promoted customer continuity and, in turn, helped blunt commoditization. By investing the time to set up a voice-mail box and by learning the system of speed-dial codes required to access, play, and delete from that box, customers effectively erected their own barriers to switching to a competitive service.

Then something unsurprising happened. In the 1990s telecoms grew enthusiastic about the lucrative nature of their ancillary offerings and began to multiply the options available.[9] Before long, they were bombarding customers with too many choices and experiencing diminishing returns from introducing new enhancements. Creating so many options had made it unwieldy for customers to evaluate.[10] Worse, as competitors mimicked each other's offers, the most important ancillaries became as easy to price-shop as the original rate cards.

The answer to so many options (now clear in retrospect) was to start rebundling products into a handful of easy-to-digest plans.[11] At the end of the decade and into the early 2000s, telecoms targeted plans at individual customer segments and tailored relevant features for each segment. For example, some bundled plans offered flat-rate calling on weekends or weeknights, or to other customers of the same carrier.[12] Telecoms offered numerous calling-plan bundles, often with relevant edge services like call-waiting, with slightly different features to meet the specific needs and calling patterns of different customers.[13] For example, they met the needs of families by discounting long-distance access rates during nights and weekends bundled with unlimited local calling and directory assistance.[14] As local and long-distance calling became more commoditized and telecoms offered unlimited calling plans, popular bundled services like call-waiting and Caller ID became important selling features.[15]

Often, the bundled edge strategy can be even more successful than the original incarnation. Instead of selecting, say, two value-added services à la carte, customers often buy the equivalent of multiple value-added services, including those they wouldn't have chosen as stand-alone services. What's more, when product edges are wrapped around the core service, they are relatively fast and easy to market.

Edge-based bundles also make value easily recognizable. In the telecom value-added services example, customers were quite happy as they perceived that they had found a solution that mapped to them specifically. By bundling edge offerings with the core, the phone companies were able to merchandise their offer with much more tailored marketing that amplified the most valuable characteristics of edge-based customization and edge-based solutions.

The telecom space has remained intensely competitive over the ensuing years, with high monthly attrition as the major players have continued to outpromote each other, buying valuable customers out of contracts in the endless quest for temporary share gains.[16] But two things are certain. First, telecom gross margins have consistently returned to 50 percent to 60 percent, again and again, over the last twenty years.[17] Second, edge strategy was critical to achieving this margin preservation in the face of strongly commoditizing forces.

The caveat here is that bundling has been around forever and will always be an important core marketing strategy. It is not always the best way to merchandise edge products that are sometimes better presented à la carte, as we saw in chapter 5. However, there is a special case when the number of edges being marketed becomes burdensome for the customer, undoing some of the good that is done by edge-based customization and edge-based solutions. In these cases, edge-based bundling can play an important role in cutting through the noise and reaching the customer again.

Perhaps the most important aspect of edge-based bundling is that it brings us full circle to a curated set of offers. As we've seen, by using these three strategic moves, companies can deconstruct and reconstruct products by slightly modifying their edges in a powerful way. This means they can (1) innovate more quickly and cheaply, (2) expand from a product sale to a more holistic solution sale, and (3) formulate or reposition variants of the solution in a more targeted way to individual customer segments.

Bringing It All Together

The three strategic moves described here work best in conjunction. Often we see a familiar pattern as companies introduce, embrace, and then actively promote ancillaries. For example, edge-based bundling amplifies the power of the edge strategies that precede and enable it. It can make it easier to understand how the choices implied by edge-based customization go together with the core product. It can make solution-focused marketing more recognizable.

Edge merchandising is a system that makes edge offerings resonate as strongly as possible with customers. With a focus on presenting the right offer to the right customer at the right time, edge tactics evolve into a cohesive marketing strategy.

Edge strategy often commences with an examination of the basics. Sometimes this involves unbundling core elements. As discussed in earlier chapters, this is the realm of inside product edge strategy. This unbundling can create a level playing field across competitors to deal with the margin compression imposed by cost creep or simply create the flexibility required to better mix offer components across different customer segments.

Then there is the careful consideration of upselling. Companies can gradually introduce various add-ons and complementary secondary products and services until each customer segment can select what it requires to satisfy its unique product needs. These are ideally based on outside product edges, benefiting from the leverage of foundational assets and often designated as enhancements to the core offer. They also include offering those inside edge elements previously stripped from the core offer so that customers who value them can add them back in.

The next step involves elevating the customer dialogue from a product decision to a mission decision. In order to move the customer's mentality from a defined permission set to a broader mission space, the company must reframe the offering from its current overlap with the customer's journey to include another step or two along a journey. By accessing journey edges, and the associated foundational assets that support them, companies can harness the power of moving from products to solutions with only incremental relative effort.

Finally, as edge offerings proliferate, companies should reconsider edge bundling. This time, the reassembling of core and edge offerings can sometimes be a means to more efficiently present the value conferred by the three preceding steps. This is done by targeting customer segments very specifically and calibrating the offers in a way that resonates with each. In this way, the core product also benefits from the power of edge offering accompaniment. This common progression can

FIGURE 7-1

The edge merchandising matrix

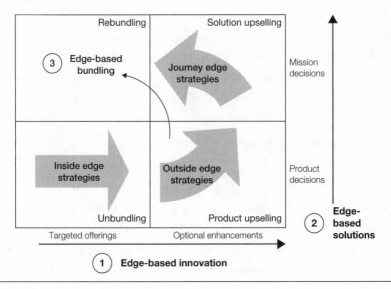

be characterized in the edge merchandising matrix (see figure 7-1). The matrix delineates the three strategic moves that make up edge merchandising and the natural roles of inside, outside, and journey edge strategies in this system of combating commoditization.

If you pursue adjacent spaces (either new products to existing customers or new customers for existing products), you are departing from your core business and taking on meaningful risk. If these are sensible bets in an efficient market, the reward for these departures should be roughly proportional to the risk absorbed. But that also assumes that there are enough bets for everything to average out. The problem is that many bets are not very sensible, or the market is not sufficiently efficient, or executives may simply not have enough chances for everything to average out.

By contrast, the power of edge economics lies precisely in its asymmetry. The amount of upside far outweighs the downside, measured in either cost or risk or both. There is no trick here, no free lunch. Part of the lunch was already paid for, so to speak, and it often sits unnoticed on the edge of the table.

Practitioner's Notes

- Introducing limited operational complexity (through ancillaries) can be a good compromise between absolute core efficiency at one end of the spectrum and highly configured offerings at the other.

- You can apply edge strategy to familiar marketing tools like customization, solution selling, and in certain cases, bundling, to provide an easier, cheaper, and highly effective method to combat commoditization.

- Edge-based customization enables product configuration without having to make fundamental changes to how you produce your core offering. When customers are involved in the final configuration choices, they become vested and, by extension, impute switching costs. Product edges are specifically valuable in this effort because they provide some of the best options to enlist customers in helping create modular offerings that resonate.

- Edge-based solutions are attractive because they are grounded in the customer journey. The art of solution marketing is to shift from individual product sales, which are necessarily transactional, to elevated discussions about helping customers complete missions. Edges are powerful auxiliaries in this effort; since they leverage foundational assets, edges help frame solutions in a way that is more natural and credible.

- When the number of edge-based options proliferates, the tyranny of choice can set in, making it harder for customers to decide and more difficult to close the sale. When this happens, edge-based bundling can be a useful construct. Essentially, this strategy boils down to wrapping multiple edge-based offerings around the core offering in a way that makes the value more recognizable to individual customer segments.

- In summary, edge-based merchandising is a holistic framework that applies the three aforementioned strategic moves in an orchestrated way. Edge offerings are often secondary in customers' considerations (after the core). Therefore, the onus is on you to present the right offer to the right customer at the right time to cut through noise and distraction. Doing this well, however, can truly tip the balance away from commoditization and back in your favor.

THE EDGE OF BIG DATA

Enabling New Ways to Create Value

One of the points we make in this book is that an edge mindset is not a new thing. Examples of edge successes are present across time and across industries. One exception, where we see the opportunity for edge strategy to be more relevant today and dramatically more relevant tomorrow, is in the context of data.

Just as with UnitedHealth in chapter 4, there are many examples of companies that have found ways to monetize their existing data in markets outside their core. The credit card issuers MasterCard, Visa, and American Express have long recognized the aggregated value of the transaction data their core businesses collect, and they use this to empower ancillary information and consulting services to business customers.[1] So does Gannett Company, an international media and marketing solutions company. It operates the job-seeker website Careerbuilder.com and aggregates the data it gleans from individual postings on the site to produce solutions for employers. These additional services include providing geographic, demographic, and economic reports on the labor market.[2]

These are illustrations of companies applying an enterprise edge strategy to data and information. They recognize that their data is an asset that has uses beyond their core business. When a company's data is useful to other companies, it can monetize the data as an edge strategy. For little incremental investment and risk, these companies leverage information they are already collecting to create new revenue streams. In fact, leveraging your data as an enterprise edge asset may be the most valuable thing you can do with it. Finding monetization opportunities like this is just one of a growing number of ways data can support edge strategies.

How Big Is Big Data?

Do you know how big a zettabyte is? It is 1,000,000,000,000,000,000,000, or 10^{21}, bytes. Why, you may wonder, do we have need for such a word? This is currently the measuring stick required to describe the world of data. At the time of this writing, EMC, an IT solutions firm, estimated the size of the digital universe to be about 4.4 zettabytes. Between now and 2020, just five years away, this number is expected to grow tenfold to 44 zettabytes.[3] Big data indeed.

Even more interesting is that only 5 percent of this data is actually being analyzed today and only 20 percent is accessible by the cloud, or "connected." In 2020, EMC predicts that up to 35 percent of data will be useful for analysis and 40 percent will be connected.[4] So, while the overall amount of data will multiply by a dizzying factor of ten, the amount of useful and accessible data could increase by a factor of more than one hundred (see figure 8-1). A key driver of the enhanced usefulness of data being created is the ability to append or tag information to the data.

This is possible thanks to the increasing contribution from so-called embedded systems. The "internet of things" is a now well-established

FIGURE 8-1

Growth of big data over time

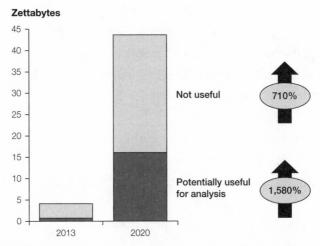

Source: Vernon Turner, David Reinsel, John F. Gantz, and Stephen Minton, "The Digital Universe of Opportunities: Rich Data and the Increasing Value of the Internet of Things," IDC and EMC Corporation, April 2014.

Note: Growth rates are rounded to the nearest ten percentage points.

moniker for such systems.[5] For example, consumer fitness aids and sleep monitors all produce tagged data. They don't just record measured results like temperature and motion, but also the time, location, and context of that recording, making it far more useful. Applications such as these are just as common in a commercial context: now medical equipment, industrial equipment, mining tools, utilities—even garbage cans—all create and upload useful data.

How to Seize the Big Data
Edge Opportunity

Big data, and the ascendency of smart and accessible information, represents an enormous opportunity for virtually any company. The massive enhancement to the visibility of how a given business and its market are performing will empower companies to be even better at delivering on their core offerings. Factories will be more automated and more integrated with marketplaces; supply chains will respond to demand in real time and, eventually, practically run themselves.

Unfortunately, big data also represents a significant challenge for many companies, requiring them to invest in becoming better at generating, capturing, storing, and analyzing data if they are to remain competitive. The internet of things is frequently cited as introducing a disruptive new competitive dynamic that will separate the digital winners from the losers.

The expansion of data and the capabilities for using it also directly increase the size of the opportunity for enterprise edge strategies. As your enterprise increases the amount and usefulness of its data, it will find more and more potential opportunities with companies that could also find value in this data, perhaps even companies in different industries and markets.

Consider how your company will be generating data in five years' time. What opportunities could this open up for your company to avail itself of an enterprise edge move? Consider your sources of data today and how these will expand over time. Also think about how your investments will make this data more useful by appending information and connecting it to the internet. As with the approach to enterprise edge strategies we detail in chapter 4, identifying data-driven edge opportunities involves similar questions:

- What are your company's different sources of data?

  - Can you list and describe them all?

- What is the quality of this data?

  - Is it well structured?

  - Is it longitudinal (over time)?

  - Is it customer-specific?

- How could this data be useful to others?

  - To your current customers or suppliers?

- Who else is affected by this data?

- Is this data relevant to any industry other than my company's?

• Who, other than your company's competitors, would buy this data?

• What value would they derive from the data?

Answering these questions is not easy. It takes a coordinated effort to break this down. What often works best is to assemble a structured working session (or several) with a cross-section of stakeholders, both internal and external to an organization. Include people adjacent to the business, like suppliers and customers, but also people completely perpendicular to your business, such as technology experts, academics, and leaders from analogous industries. Facilitating a workshop to work through these questions and challenge the conventional wisdom can be extremely effective at unlocking avenues for possible enterprise edge opportunities.

Based on our research and client work, we have made some observations about the expanding opportunity for data-powered edge strategies that can help you identify where you will want to focus:

1. The usefulness of data is indiscriminate.

2. Data fluency, or the ability to analyze and understand data, is increasing.

3. Data is a product.

4. Consumers value data, too.

5. Renting data to other users is easy.

6. The value of data can be disproportionately large for users outside your enterprise.

Usefulness Is Indiscriminate

Our first observation is that the usefulness of data is not unilateral. Big data is not uniquely directed at being useful for your business alone. Making your data smarter and more accessible for internal use makes it more useful for others, too. This expanded connectedness of data is directly applicable to opening up new edge opportunities.

This type of investment also expands the range of other users for which the data could be of value. In the context of enterprise edges, this conclusion is important. As data becomes smarter and more accessible, your opportunities to find enterprise edge opportunities for your data should increase.

In our review of over six hundred of the largest global companies, we found a wealth of examples of data being sold across industries. One company that understands this concept is the Toyota Motor Company.

In 2013, Toyota launched a business solution for municipal and business customers in Japan that allowed its customers to access real-time traffic information and associated analysis. The service leveraged an existing Toyota data asset: the real-time information it collects about car location, speed, and so on from its GPS-enabled vehicles in order to support Toyota's factory-installed navigation systems. This data, called telematics, is a powerful asset, the value of which is not uniquely aligned to supporting in-car navigation.[6]

Toyota's big insight was to recognize that the data was of value to other, different customers. And importantly, the strategy acknowledged that allowing others to have access to the data would not affect the current core purpose enabling the navigation service. Toyota's enterprise edge service takes real-time traffic information generated from telematics data about vehicle location, travel speed, and other parameters to provide a cloud-based information service for a monthly fee starting at nearly $2,000.[7]

There are many different ways in which Toyota's businesses and government customers use this edge service. Many use the data to study and improve traffic flow, provide map information and routing services, and assist in emergency response efforts. Owners of large commercial vehicle fleets can use the service to track the location of their vehicles and their progress in completing delivery routes. There is even a consumer-focused offering, Toyota's subscription-based G-Book smartphone app, which uses the telematics information to advise individual drivers on the most efficient routes so they can avoid traffic and other delays.[8]

Data Fluency Is Increasing

A second conclusion is that in this new data-driven world, more and more companies will be ready for analysis. If, as we implied earlier, data management and analysis are fast becoming table-stakes capabilities for competing in your core market, then more companies can find value in data or, more properly, in *your* company's data. This increases the number of possible customers you can find for your data offerings. The most immediately interesting cohort to consider is your existing customers. Cargill, the diversified food and agriculture company, recognized this opportunity.

Cargill's core business is to sell crop seeds and other crop-related products to farmers and then to buy the resulting grain and commodities and either trade them or process and distribute them to food manufacturers.[9] In 2014 the company unveiled a new data product designed to help farmers increase crop yields. NextField DataRx is a software product that guides farmers on how best to plant their fields using so-called prescriptive planning technology. The software, which Cargill sells separately from its base products and services, takes account of 250 variables, including soil type, environmental condition, and seed performance. Cargill claims that the technology will help boost yields by as much as 10 percent. "We're trying to help farmers maximize their [return on] investment and the output of their farm," said Steve Becraft, crop-inputs manager for Cargill's agriculture business.[10]

The company developed NextField DataRx to complement its core service of buying and selling seed, and other agricultural products. The software package leverages the company's strong foundational assets in agricultural know-how and market relationships. In its core business of seed development and marketing, Cargill accumulated a large database of information detailing how its seeds performed in various types of soil and weather conditions. Turning this information around, the company realized that it would be able to analyze a farmer's land and provide greater predictive certainty for previously unknown but critically important outcomes like crop yields and pesticide effectiveness. This was the key insight in developing the NextField DataRx software—that Cargill could use its already developed database that supported seed development to advise its customers in their own businesses.[11]

Once Cargill had developed the software, bringing it to market was only a small incremental effort, but produced highly profitable returns, given the recurring nature of the revenue and its minimal cost of delivery. This strategy demonstrates a number of hallmarks of edge thinking. First, it is consistent with product edge strategy: Cargill found a way to append a value-added service to its seed crop offering. Second, it can be seen as an enterprise edge move because Cargill is availing itself of existing data and knowledge assets in providing the service to farmers.

A critical conclusion from this example is that a key enabler of the opportunity for Cargill was that its customers were ready and willing to use the data.

Data Is a Product

An expanded fluency in data and an increasing ability to make it useful mean that more and more companies and customers have a need for data. The internet of things is affecting not only the consumer world, but also almost every industry, resulting in a business environment where most core product offerings can include a data service of some kind.

Caterpillar, which makes earth-moving vehicles and other heavy machinery, understands this. For several years, it has provided its mining customers with technology that helps improve fleet utilization, productivity, safety, and regulatory compliance. Now, it is starting to offer this package of technology under the brand "Cat Connect" in each of its end markets.[12]

Caterpillar now factory-installs sensors and other computerized equipment in many of its vehicles. It can then offer an optional product-edge data service to its customers, allowing customers to monitor how their vehicles are performing, when they need maintenance, and so on. Most vehicles have the technology installed at the factory. For an additional monthly service charge, Caterpillar customers can unlock the flow of data via a subscription to the Cat Connect service. To many customers, this is a small cost relative to the initial capital investment in the machinery. For Caterpillar, the economic impact is much larger. This data-driven product edge creates a valuable recurring revenue stream for Caterpillar and serves to strengthen its relationship with customers. Furthermore, because the equipment is factory-installed and the software is already written, the Cat Connect service produces a higher margin than the company's capital-intensive core equipment sales.[13]

Consumers Value Data

Data fluency is empowering not only business-to-business companies. We see a similar dynamic in consumer-facing markets. By 2020, the millennial generation—those born after 1982—will represent the largest consumer-spending group in the United States.[14] This generation and the one after it (Gen Z) have never known a world without the internet; their adult lives are immersed in the world of cellphones and social media. These are truly the technology generations.

Mobile technology, in particular, has empowered these consumers to be ready and willing to interface with data in all shapes and forms. As our consumer-facing clients tell us, understanding and taking advantage of the permission to engage with this generation through technology is a focus in virtually every aspect of their businesses today.

Consumer-facing companies have opportunities to target data-enabled product edges. As you race to invest in technology to connect with your consumer digitally through mobile apps, websites, social media, and onsite technologies such as kiosks and touch screens, consider how a data service can append to your core offer. Certainly there are numerous ways data can enhance a core offering: "the sale is starting now," "your departure gate has changed," "your room is ready for check-in," "a table has opened up in the restaurant," "the wait time in the line is currently ten minutes," and so on.

As we detailed in chapter 5 on effective upselling, before you weave these new features into your core offering, pause and consider where you can present these add-ons as options that you can charge for separately. If this seems challenging, ask yourself if you can offer levels for free (for example, a basic information feed) and an enhanced premium service for which you can charge an upgrade fee.

For example, let's examine LinkedIn, the business-oriented social media service that was launched in May 2003.[15] At the time of writing, LinkedIn claimed to have over 364 million members in over 200 countries worldwide.[16] Membership on LinkedIn is free. The basic membership, like most social media tools, allows a member to build a profile and use it to cultivate and interact with a network of professional connections globally.[17] It is a truly amazing and modern tool for maintaining contact information with both friends and business connections. Millennials don't own Rolodexes.

LinkedIn was first listed on the NASDAQ in 2011 and now, at the time of writing, has revenues of over $2 billion and a market capitalization of $29 billion.[18] The bulk of this revenue-generating business, what we would consider its core, addresses enterprise customers with talent-sourcing and marketing services. But 20 percent of its revenue comes from its members.[19] LinkedIn recognized that some of its members wanted access to more information and that they would be willing to pay for it. Starting at $29.99 a month, premium members can see the full list of members who viewed their profiles in the last ninety days, send three InMail messages that allow them to contact anyone on LinkedIn, view the full profiles of people three connections away in their networks, and perform advanced searches. The premium product offerings are targeted at specific types of users with special add-ons for each: the Job Seeker, Business Plus, Sales Navigator Professional, and Recruiter Lite.[20]

This member-generated portion of LinkedIn's revenues provides a great example of a data-enabled edge upsell. While super-users account for 20 percent of LinkedIn's revenue, estimates put the number of these premium subscribers at only a tiny proportion of its membership.[21] To earn this revenue, LinkedIn is leveraging its existing data assets; the information and enhanced functionality are already present in the network. The premium offers are optional add-ons on top of the base service; they exist at the edge of the core product and are targeted at specific but existing customers. And the options generate incremental revenue, critical for an edge strategy.

Renting Data to Others Is Easy

Not all companies are champing at the bit to embrace this new standard of data fluency and analytical strength. For some, possibly many, big data is actually a daunting prospect. Or perhaps equally often, while management teams have the vision and eagerness to access all that big data has to offer, companies are disappointed to realize that their existing equipment and systems are major impediments to achieving their big data dreams. Other companies acknowledge that they simply don't have the in-house talent and expertise to capitalize on the opportunity.

When faced with these challenges, we see another opportunity for an edge mindset to be valuable. Perhaps a company cannot fully realize the value of its data, but by assessing the possibilities of who would rent its data, the firm may find new ways to capture its value without having to become a data expert. That is, by activating an enterprise edge strategy, the company may be able to monetize a valuable asset (its data) in new and creative ways.

Our view of the post–big data world is therefore less binary than you may have concluded based on the dynamics we described at the beginning of this chapter. Instead of a world where winners are defined purely by their level of data management and analytical prowess, and by contrast, the companies without these competencies are the losers, we envision another path to success for companies that *rent* their data to others. These data renters will recognize that the power of their data is not limited by how they can use it to enable their own core business; they can also benefit by letting others access its power. And the value may be far greater in these cases; in fact, employing an enterprise edge approach to data is likely to be a far more accessible (and potentially valuable) use of data assets for the majority of companies.

We can see this phenomenon in the example of UnitedHealth that we described in chapter 4. In order to operate its core health insurance business profitably, UnitedHealth collected a vast quantity of information on its subscribers' health outcomes over time. This database was table stakes for the company's underwriting business; it would be nearly impossible to earn a profit in its core health insurance division without tracking subscribers' health outcomes over time.

Despite this, UnitedHealth was certainly not a clinical research expert. To use this type of longitudinal data in a clinical context, UnitedHealth would have needed to develop deep expertise in a number of disciplines unrelated to insurance—biostatistics, chemistry and biology, drug development, and regulatory approval, to name a few. Instead of investing in building these complicated (and expensive) new competencies, UnitedHealth decided to rent anonymized subscriber data to pharmaceutical and biotech companies, which already had deep expertise in these areas.

From this example, we see clear evidence supporting the theory that big data does not produce binary winners and losers, dictated only by analytical sophistication. UnitedHealth was able to rent (and monetize) its data assets without becoming an expert in clinical analytics; furthermore, its customers were able to extract a tremendous amount of value from the rented data.

Data's Value Can Be Disproportionate

Your company's data is often more valuable to other companies than it is to you. Many companies consume themselves trying to drive breakthrough insights for their core business from data. The value often comes incrementally through a series of small wins.

However, when you make your data available to outsiders in different industries, you can potentially multiply its value. Your data could be the *missing link* for a company that has never had access to the side of your customers that only you see or the perspective over time that your business model allows. Even data that may seem trivial to your business, when seen longitudinally over time, could be a prism of insight for another company. For Toyota, simple information about a driver's trip to the grocery store, once assembled across many similar errands, provides a rich perspective for government agencies focused on improving road safety and reducing congestion.

The asymmetry in this edge opportunity is worth emphasizing. While the attraction of edge strategy is the accessibility and immediacy of opportunities, the benefits, while valuable, are often incremental to your core business. Fortunately, this is not necessarily so with data, creating a compelling reason why data should be one of the first places you look when seeking edge opportunities.

Practitioner's Notes

- Data is a valuable enterprise asset that readily enables enterprise edge opportunities due, in part, to the fact that it is unconstrained; letting someone else access your data doesn't diminish its value.

- Data is also one of the easiest tools to use in a product edge opportunity; virtually any product or service can be enhanced with associated data and information. The data could be about how the product is performing or how a customer can make the most of the product or service.

- Opportunities for both enterprise edge and product edge strategies using data should increase because:

  - The amount of data being creating is expanding massively.

  - The portion of data that is useful is also set to increase.

  - Companies are becoming more data literate and reliant.

  - Consumers and products are becoming more technologically enabled.

- Data analysis proficiency is not a requirement of data-enabled edge strategies. Using an edge mindset to find ways to rent your data should help you capture some of its value, even if your company is not strongly analytical.

- The value of data is both indiscriminant and disproportionate. That is, there is no limit to the number of potential customers for your data, and there is no limit to how valuable your data could be to these users.

- We recommend that companies search their data as one of the first places to go for edge opportunities. Look to your customers; they might value your edge offerings. But also look further afield; the key to many enterprise edge strategies (for which data is often a key input) is to consider who, besides your current customers, could find value in your data assets.

- Your data often has disproportionate value outside your enterprise. For most companies, analyzing internal data produces only incremental insights. However, when companies employ an enterprise edge mindset and find new, external uses for data, the value can be enormous, both in terms of insight and financial returns.

CHAPTER 9

A NEW MINDSET FOR M&A

Getting Real Value from Synergies

This transaction is another major milestone in creating a new ICI for the new century. The portfolio of businesses in ICI is well positioned to develop and deliver sustainable profitable growth over the coming years.

—Charles Miller Smith, CEO, ICI PLC

Imperial Chemical Industries (ICI PLC) was a pillar of British industry. Founded in 1926 through the merger of four companies, it was the largest manufacturer in Britain for much of its history. ICI competed with the likes of DuPont in the production of a broad range of industrial chemicals, polymers, fertilizers, explosives, and paints worldwide. ICI patented more than thirty-three thousand inventions over its seventy-five-year history, including products like Polyester and Perspex.[1]

In the summer of 1997, with a market capitalization of $9.4 billion and under the leadership of CEO Charles Miller Smith (a former director at Unilever), ICI acquired a series of specialty chemical companies from Unilever for $8 billion.[2] This move was a bold effort to transform the company and reposition it away from the cyclical bulk products of its core and toward higher-margin, higher-growth businesses.[3] The company took on $8.5 billion in debt to fund the deal, for which many observers felt it overpaid.[4] To complete the transformation, the company endeavored to sell off all of its commodity businesses over the next three years.[5] It achieved this sell-off, but at discounted prices.[6]

Unfortunately, the strategy did not pan out as expected. By 2003, ICI's market capitalization had cratered to less than $2 billion.[7] By 2006, in an effort to repay the remaining debt, it was forced to sell most of the specialty businesses it originally bought from Unilever.[8] After this, all that remained was the paint business, which was bought out by Akzo Nobel, a Dutch paint firm, in 2008.[9] ICI was no more.

The Siren Song

Merger and acquisition (M&A) transactions are popular. Data shows that up to forty thousand M&A transactions occur globally each year (see figure 9-1). The aggregate value of these deals varies between $2 trillion and $4 trillion, depending on the year.[10] On this basis, it is fair to say that you may have had firsthand experience with some level of M&A strategy in action: you may have worked for a company that was acquired, or perhaps you are in business development for your company and have orchestrated deals yourself. It will come as no surprise to learn that making an M&A transaction successful is hard.

So hard, in fact, that most deals fail. Our firm regularly reviews the performance of the M&A deal market and publishes the findings. Depending on the time period, they will tell you that anywhere from

FIGURE 9-1

Number and value of worldwide M&A transactions

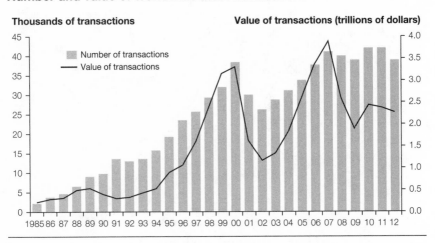

60 percent to 80 percent of deals fail to create shareholder value, and many actually destroy value instead. Their analysis shows that for more than twenty-five hundred deals conducted from 1993 to 2010—a period that included two boom-and-bust economic cycles—the average total shareholder return two years postdeal was reduced by 10 percent, and that 60 percent of those deals actually destroyed value (see figure 9-2).[11]

M&A Is Not a Strategy

Why, you may ask, with such poor odds, do companies continue to see M&A as such a compelling strategic option?

In our experience, companies undertake M&A transactions for a wide variety of reasons, some good and some less so: meet sales objectives, grow earnings per share, deny a competitor, enhance skills, diversify risk, obtain assets, gain strategic advantage, maintain independence, or even for bragging rights. But, despite all this, it is important

FIGURE 9-2

M&A performance: acquirers' cumulative total shareholder returns

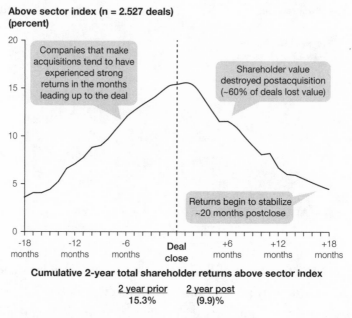

Above sector index (n = 2.527 deals)
(percent)

Companies that make acquisitions tend to have experienced strong returns in the months leading up to the deal

Shareholder value destroyed postacquisition (~60% of deals lost value)

Returns begin to stabilize ~20 months postclose

-18 months   -12 months   -6 months   **Deal close**   +6 months   +12 months   +18 months

Cumulative 2-year total shareholder returns above sector index

2 year prior	2 year post
15.3%	(9.9)%

Source: CAPIQ data; L.E.K. analysis.

Note: All deals were greater than $50 million in transaction value, were 100% control transactions, and were completed during the 1993–2010 period by public acquirers; the US was the primary location of the acquirer and target; acquirers' total shareholder returns were compared against S&P 500 sector and composite indexes to normalize for market-related performance (S&P 500 composite index was used in the earlier sample years before sector indexes were created); excludes REITs.

to remember that M&A is a *tool* for strategy, not a strategy in and of itself. As such, it is the strategy *behind the deal* that matters.

We recognize two main culprits behind virtually all deals that fail:

- The buyer overpaid.

- The postdeal integration was poorly executed.

In our experience, once a deal is consummated, successful integration is determined by the quality of the postdeal process: strong leadership, a methodological approach, broad organizational buy-in, and focus on the value drivers. Successful integrations have dedicated integration teams, robust planning, a focus on overcommunicating, and well-planned talent-retention strategies.

Postdeal integration is a topic for another book. Here, we will focus on what happens before the deal: how the buyer can ensure it is isolating the deals that will be successful, and how it can avoid getting the price for those deals wrong.

All in the Price

What should you pay for a company? Three factors go into determining the value of a company to shareholders:

- The free cash flow profile that the company expects to generate from its operations over the short to medium term.

- The long-term time horizon for the company (and how those prospects affect the terminal or residual value).

- The risk, or the level of uncertainty, around the two preceding variables and the associated discount that accounts for it.

Conventional investment strategy follows a simple principle: find the highest value use for all assets. If the value of one of your assets is greater to others than it is to you, you should strongly consider selling the asset. This is where the concept of synergies comes in. Synergy is the term for the value that is created in a transaction. It can come from rationalizing costs that are duplicated across the organizations, costs such as labor, production assets, the sales force, and management teams. It can come from scale efficiencies, such as increased purchasing power. Then there are revenue synergies.

Revenue synergies are typically the hardest part of a predeal valuation to get right. They stem from the heart of the strategy behind a deal. When the buyer is betting that it can improve the commercial outcomes for one or both entities as a result of the deal, it is fundamentally betting on revenue synergies. We find most companies get it wrong.

How an Edge Approach Can Help

If a sound strategy is the key to ensuring the success of a deal, and if an edge mindset can be powerful in formulating such a strategy, what role can edge strategy play in M&A? We have found that edge strategy can be extremely helpful in M&A for the same reasons that it can position your company for success in its organic growth strategies—namely, helping you to make decisions that are lower risk, have a higher probability of success, require less investment, and generate higher margins by leveraging existing assets.

The edge framework focuses a manager on where her products fail to align with customer needs. It forces a manager to understand her customer's journey. It challenges a manager to consider how a separate enterprise can deploy her company's assets.

Let us review the edge framework and discuss how to apply it to M&A decisions.

1. Product edge applications. When companies explore a potential deal, they first examine the acquiring company and clearly define the company's core offerings; it is important to examine each core offering separately in this process.

This examination leads us to the first key point to highlight: revenue synergies typically come from the interactions of core *offerings*, not companies. Take, for example, a hotel. You might say that it has one core offering: hotel rooms for travelers. But it might also offer meeting and event services to businesses. This product is very different; the customer is also different.

At the edge of each of these core offerings, in between what is currently offered and what customers give permission to offer, we can examine how a potential transaction would be accretive. This involves a very precise investigation of how the acquirer could add additional features or services by drawing on the target's products and services.

Recognizing where such a product edge opportunity exists allows us to form the basis of a revenue synergy estimate. We must apply the same scrutiny to the target, asking what exactly are its core offerings and specifically what customers do the offerings serve. If our acquirer's products and services can logically append to the target's offerings, then we have good grounding for another synergistic opportunity.

Take, for example, when a hotel chain acquires a beauty-care brand, such as in 2004 when Starwood Hotels & Resorts Worldwide acquired the Bliss brand from LVMH. This type of product edge acquisition can generate a number of synergies, as the hotel provides access to its customers though new points of sale for the lotions and creams in the spa and, perhaps, a lobby boutique. But the brand can also be used for in-room amenities as part of the hotel's core offering, which provides greater exposure to new potential customers. "It's a perfect fit . . . an obvious platform for us—as a still fledgling beauty brand—to get our products into the hands of a very targeted market of travelers," said Marcia Kilgore, Bliss's founder, of the deal.[12]

As with any product edge strategy, this analysis must consider customer segments independently and how each is served by the various core offerings. Not all customers will value all options; failing to adequately examine the needs of each customer segment could mean missing an opportunity. At the same time, insufficiently considering each customer segment's needs may result in an overestimation of synergy opportunities by failing to identify which customers will not recognize the value.

This methodical process of mapping core offerings to customer permission sets, one by one, looks for asymmetries that could indicate an edge. Critically, if the analysis does not identify any product edge opportunities from a potential deal, it should raise a red flag that revenue synergies may not exist in the transaction.

Product edges are also the first place to look when identifying possible targets. Many deals are executed on the basis that they will provide access to new customers. Product edge strategy adds needed discipline by asking, "Is the product or service being cross-sold sufficiently related to the acquirer's core business?" If not, then the risk that the new customer will not give you permission to sell the new service—a common flaw in deals justified on this basis—is high.

Filtering for situations where the cross-sell opportunities are more natural product edges, versus big commercial leaps, is a great way to reduce the risk in the pitfalls of finding synergistic targets.

2. Journey edge applications. The customers of both the target and the acquirer should be studied in the context of their journeys. As detailed in chapter 3, it is important to identify opportunities to slightly expand participation on a customer's journey.

- What is the end-to-end journey of each customer segment relative to each core offering (of both the target and the acquirer)?

- Do the offers of either company help to complete more of the journey of any of these identified customer segments?

- Again, if this analysis fails to identify a meaningful overlap, then the odds of finding significant revenue synergies decrease.

When screening for acquisition targets, the journey edge framework can be used as well. What activities does the company undertake and what other products or services does it encounter along the way? If a target can provide the capability to engage in such activities or is already offering these services, there is greater potential to create revenue synergies.

3. Enterprise edge applications. As explained in chapter 4, the enterprise edge can be the most complex, but is often the most valuable source of edge strategy. In the context of a deal, this is also true. Recall that an enterprise edge strategy is one that takes advantage of the existing foundational assets of your company when they can be readily leveraged as a new service or product offering. In assessing a transaction, a similar approach can be used to identify enterprise edge-based synergies. This begins with an audit of the foundational assets of each company.

- Do the companies produce any form of by-products?

- Where can they access spare capacity?

- Are there opportunities to rent out unconstrained assets?

Any identified target that can benefit from these enterprise edges may create not only revenue synergies, but also cost synergies. It is also possible for one company's foundational assets to append to the offering of another company in the form of a product or journey edge. This is especially true for intangible assets like knowledge and data (as detailed in chapter 8).

Summary of Edge-Based Acquisition Analysis

Acquisition strategy in the context of existing assets is not unique to edge strategy. An edge approach merely adds a much sharper discipline of challenging whether assets are truly and readily useful to another company. If it is not apparent how easy it would be for a company to avail itself of your foundational assets, then synergy may prove elusive (see table 9-1).

Is it valid to consider edge strategy in any deal situation? We would argue that it is. As detailed earlier, the edge framework provides a perspective and discipline for assessing a deal that increases the likelihood you will execute with success. Is it possible for a deal to succeed that fails to meet the criteria? Certainly. However, we would challenge you, if you find yourself in such a situation (a deal that has no edge strategy

TABLE 9-1

How edge strategy can help in M&A

	Product edge analysis	Journey edge analysis	Enterprise edge analysis
Where can I find good targets to acquire?	✓	✓	
How can I prioritize possible targets?	✓	✓	✓
Where will I find revenue synergies in this deal?	✓	✓	✓
Will I be able to cross-sell products?	✓	✓	
Will I be able to find cost synergies?			✓
How difficult will it be to realize synergies?	✓	✓	✓

basis), to consider the wisdom and appropriateness of any potential transaction.

We will now apply the approach to the ICI example we introduced at the beginning of this chapter. ICI's acquisition from Unilever involved several different types of businesses, notably some that served consumer goods companies with products like starches and flavorings. Recall that ICI's core offering was commodity chemicals. The customers of these products (plastics, rubbers, bulk chemicals) were a wide array of industrial and manufacturing companies. It is clear that none of these customers had a need for food ingredients. The fast-moving consumer goods companies that purchased Unilever's products also had little need for ICI's core commodity chemical offerings.[13] So there appeared to be no compelling rationale for product edge opportunities in the deal. Unfortunately, considering the transaction through a customer journey lens leads to a similar conclusion and does not introduce any further edge-driven opportunities either.

Taking an enterprise edge view, it was possible that some know-how and expertise could theoretically be leveraged across the businesses. But, as with all technology-based companies, this know-how is highly specific and, in this case, turned out not to be especially transferable between the firms.

The reality is that this deal was not one that ICI predicated on anything like an edge strategy. The deal was absent of any of the aforementioned benefits. The strategy was to diversify, but when ICI couldn't do that fast enough, it did not have fundamental deal synergies to fall back on.

Let's now consider a different, more successful example.

A Dream Deal with Many Edges

In October 2005, Procter & Gamble (P&G) closed a deal to acquire the Gillette Company. An examination of the company's stock price reveals that this was a great success (see figure 9-3).

FIGURE 9-3

P&G-Gillette merger

P&G indexed* market stock price performance (percent)

Positive Q1 2007 results reported, September 18, 2007

P&G raises FY08 outlook, October 30, 2007

Sells brand to satisfy antitrust, September 22, 2005

Deal finalized, October 4, 2005

Initial merger announcement, January 27, 2005

Positive 2007 expectations announced, August 2, 2006

30 days prior to bid announcement (December 2004)

3 years after announcement (January 2008)

Source: Press reports, Reuters, Google Finance, analyst reports, L.E.K. analysis.

*Stock prices indexed to December 27, 2004, close value.

What was behind this success? It wasn't the acquirer's ability to negotiate an abnormally low purchase price. P&G paid a fairly standard 20 percent premium over the market value of Gillette at the time of closing.[14] The answer is that P&G justified the deal based on expected long-term synergies, both cost and revenue.

Initial reaction from the investment community was overwhelmingly positive. Warren Buffett, who was the largest shareholder in Gillette at the time, called it a "dream deal [to] create the greatest consumer-products company in the world." P&G informed the public that the transaction created "future upside potential to its double-digit annual earnings growth target." Wall Street analysts agreed. "[This is] a brilliant move strategically," wrote Linda Bolton Weiser of Oppenheimer & Co.[15]

The reason for this optimism was that it was immediately clear that the managers at P&G and Gillette—armed with insight that is central to both product and journey edge strategy—could offer something to each other's customers. Sure, both companies were in the personal-care industry. But P&G's core was soaps and creams with a focus on female consumers; Gillette, of course, was a razor company, focused on men.[16] The deal makers recognized that by using P&G's product development expertise and production capabilities, it could expand the range of products marketed under the Gillette brand. Shave lotions, deodorants, shower gels—all targeted the male consumer; all leveraged P&G's product technology and expertise.

This synergy went both ways. Gillette truly was a leader in blade technology and had been rewarded in the market with the runaway success of its Mach series of products. Combining this with P&G's lotion products, the new company was able to market Gillette's Venus razor brand for women with P&G's Olay skin-care brand as a combination product.[17]

Both companies focused on different consumer segments, but by studying the journeys of each other's customers (men's grooming and women's personal care and beauty), managers at both companies recognized three things. First, each company was not fully completing its customers' journeys. Consumers were using other products in combination with its offering; for example, Gillette users also used after-shave lotions. Second, each company's core offering could play a direct role helping complete each other's customer journey. In the aforementioned example, P&G is an expert in the skin-care technology required to complete the shaving experience. Finally, P&G and Gillette recognized that their brands' complementary strength gave them the permission to expand their collective footprint in the customers' journeys.

These hit on all three of the edge types. Enterprise assets were leveraged in product design capabilities transferred. Product edge opportunities were captured by appending features to current products. Journey edge thinking was also used in adding products that extended their involvement in completing the consumer mission.

This wasn't the only area of synergy in the deal; a further product edge–related synergy was also a key to the merger's success. In addition to an important amount of cost synergy through rationalization, increased supplier strength, and removal of duplicated functions, the deal helped both companies in their geographic expansion goals.[18]

The deal has held up over time and justified management's expectations. Examining the acquisition four years later, professor Rosabeth Moss Kanter singled out the deal as one of her "mergers that stick," noting that "P&G met cost and revenue targets within the first year, incorporated Gillette processes considered superior to P&G's, and continued to position itself for overall growth even as the [2008–2009] recession loomed."[19]

"Roll-Ups" Using an Edge Mindset

NAVEX Global, an Oregon-based software company focused on corporate governance, risk, and compliance software, provides another example of how to effectively apply an edge mindset in identifying revenue synergies. The company offers a suite of services including compliance policy management, whistle-blowing hotlines, and other solutions designed to monitor workplace behavior.[20]

NAVEX executed a series of "roll-up" transactions from 2010 through 2012.[21] This ultimately resulted in an opportunity to achieve revenue synergies by cross-selling new products and services to existing customers of the various constituent companies. NAVEX itself was a rebranding of four separate software companies, each with a distinct offering and role in its corporate customers' compliance and ethics journey.[22] During the roll-up into a single $100 million entity in 2012, NAVEX's CEO Mark Reed articulated to the marketplace what was essentially the potential for an edge-driven cross-selling strategy.[23] In Reed's words, "[C]ollectively, the merged companies offer an unmatched level of experience and knowledge with a broad and complementary set of technology and content solutions to help global customers manage risk."[24]

Key to NAVEX's success in these deals was that it employed the same methodology present in product and journey edge analysis prior to banking on the cross-selling opportunities that underpinned the deals. It knew it was dealing with the same customers and that the offers of each acquired company were on the edges of each other's product offerings, making upselling a possibility. A further transaction helped to expand NAVEX's role on the customer journey when it acquired PolicyTech, which produced a tool for managing cases that result from compliance breaches.[25]

The financial markets were believers in NAVEX's edge strategy, too. In 2014, the company was sold for a reported $500 million to a private equity investor.[26]

Connection Failed: Revenue Synergies without an Edge

At the beginning of this chapter, we introduced the idea that making a successful transaction is hard, and even harder when it relies on revenue synergies. Now we examine a high-profile revenue synergy failure to see where edge strategy could have provided guidance.

In 2005, eBay, the online marketplace giant, bought Skype for $2.6 billion, plus the potential for a $1.4 billion performance-based milestone. At the time, Skype was a category-leading technology start-up with its offering of global internet-based video phone service.[27]

When announcing the acquisition to investors, Meg Whitman, eBay's CEO, declared that "by combining Skype with eBay and PayPal [an earlier eBay acquisition] we can create an unparalleled e-commerce and communications engine for buyers and sellers around the world . . . Communication is at the heart of community and e-commerce, making Skype a natural fit for eBay."[28]

eBay's rationale for the deal heavily centered on the idea that Skype would complement its core business. It reasoned that enabling eBay's existing customers to talk to each other in real time would make trans-actions easier and quicker.[29] This revenue synergy strategy was an effort to expand participation on the customers' journey by connecting customers with a low-cost video phone service.

"Skype can accelerate the velocity of trade on eBay and accelerate the volume of payments through PayPal, while at the same time opening up some new lines of business and creating significant new monetization opportunities for the company," Whitman explained. "We think Skype is a leap forward in online communications."[30]

Indeed, Skype and IP-based voice and video conferencing, in general, were a leap forward in online communication. Unfortunately for eBay, this had little to do with the online auctions business, and the deal itself turned out to be a disaster. The critical error was that eBay failed to both properly assess the customers' permission set and truly vet the way those customers' journeys were likely to unfold. It did not recognize that video chatting wasn't a priority for its customers; they didn't need, or particularly want, to video chat with each other in the context of an eBay transaction.[31] The result was that eBay took a $1.4 billion charge in 2007 related to Skype and sold the majority of its ownership to private investors in 2009 (see figure 9-4).[32]

If eBay had challenged its revenue synergy–based investment thesis from the perspective of edge strategy, we think it would have seen these red flags in advance. By completing a product edge assessment of its core offering, it would have explored separately each of its customer groups, both sellers and buyers, and mapped the permission sets of each. Exploring and engaging its customers' use of the core eBay offering should have alerted it to whether those customers had a need for such a step change in the velocity of their transactions. Sure, eBay might have had a need for this, but were the buyers and sellers crying out that they couldn't transact fast enough? It's unlikely that many customers were.

A study of these customers' journeys should have also brought the insight that the usage of video chat in supporting transactions was low. Indeed, the technology already existed; if this functionality was truly a

FIGURE 9-4

eBay's acquisition of Skype

eBay indexed* market
stock price performance
(percent)

Initial purchase talks, August 9, 2005

Q1 & Q2 2006 forecasts below analysts', January 18, 2006

CEO resigns and weaker 2008 forecasted, January 23, 2008

Skype acquisition finalized for $2.6B, October 14, 2005

Raised 2006 outlook, October 18, 2006

Upcoming Skype IPO announced, April 14, 2009

Low Q3 2006 estimates announced, July 19, 2006

30 days prior to bid announcement (July 2005)

Current (September 2009)

Source: Press reports, Reuters, Google Finance, analyst reports, L.E.K. analysis.

*Stock prices indexed to July 5, 2005, close value.

valuable part of the customer journey, then there should have already been evidence of widespread usage in this context. But there wasn't. Buyers weren't jumping on Skype in large numbers to engage with eBay sellers during deals; why should they do so after the deal?

Turning to Skype, a diligent manager would have found even less synergy. Skype's, and eBay's, customers were executing on entirely different missions: connecting with family and friends in the first instance, and buying and selling goods online in the second. It is hard to see how these customers would have a compelling, unmet need to facilitate transactions with family and friends while participating in Skype's core communications–focused offering.

The reality was that there was not enough synergy in the deal, and as such, eBay could not support the premium it paid for the company. eBay had bought a communication asset, unrelated to its core offering and, worse still, one whose core proposition was not on its customers' journey. The discipline of an edge approach would have helped eBay recognize this.

Blockbusters and Bolt-ons: Edge Discipline Wins in Health-Care Deals

An edge mindset can also help explain the relative successes—and failures—of some of the biggest powerhouses in the health-care industry. Observers of that industry will be familiar with the shifting complexion of its key players. At the turn of the last century, all the accolades went to the big pharmaceutical companies, "big pharma." Big-name branded drugs were making billions of dollars for the likes of Pfizer, Astra Zeneca, GSK, Bristol-Myers Squibb, Merck & Co., and Novartis. These so-called blockbuster drugs—drugs that typically net more than $1 billion in annual sales—were the focus of nearly all strategic initiatives. Pfizer alone went to market with eight of these drugs in 2000: Lipitor, Norvasc, Zoloft, Neurontin, Celebrex, Zithromax, Viagra, and Diflucan.[33]

This focus promoted an approach to acquisitions based on the blockbuster strategy, too. The central concern among big pharma executives at the time was "how can we fill the development pipeline with more blockbusters?" They, of course, hoped that the in-house research and development teams would produce some hits, but in order to maintain a constant revenue growth story for investors, the executives also realized that they needed some help from outside to fill in the gaps. This is where transactions came in. And when you consider that the largest big pharma companies at the time, Pfizer and GSK, each had global revenues in excess of $20 billion in 2000, you can see that some of those gaps can be very enormous.[34]

The result was a lot of transaction activity. Big pharma got bigger but, as a side effect, also broader, picking up consumer health businesses, animal health products, and nutrition assets from others and from each other as part of these blockbuster deals.[35] At some stage, you could argue that acquisitions, which were supposedly an activity designed to support the core by filling in product line gaps, had become the core business itself. And one that was not sustainable. Since 2012, the industry has spoken of big pharma slimming down, with many of these transactions being reversed as players trade noncore assets back to players for which they are a better fit.[36]

From an edge perspective, these moves broke the rules. The transactions took the acquirers into new markets with new customers unrelated to their existing product offerings. And just like Charles Miller Smith at ICI, big pharma entered into businesses unrelated to, and therefore unable to leverage, their foundational assets or customer relationships. While some of this diversification was collateral damage due to the pursuit of blockbusters, the moves were certainly not taken with an edge mindset.

But, you may argue, the mega-companies were looking to fill mega-gaps in the growth expectations. Is restricting your focus to your edge sufficient? In order to grow at this scale, do you need to employ a diversification strategy, not just incremental moves? The case of Gilead and other so-called biotech companies suggests otherwise.

Gilead Sciences was founded in 1987 by twenty-nine-year-old Dr. Michael Riordan, with a $2 million investment by Menlo Ventures.[37] Today, Gilead has revenues of $20 billion and a market cap of $148 billion.[38] Gilead is what would be described today as a "big biotech." In contrast to the big pharma companies, Gilead and its peers use biotechnology in their core business. This distinction relates to how they each make their drugs.[39]

But the distinction doesn't stop there. Nearly all biotechs like Gilead grew from start-ups over the last twenty years.[40] And they have a very different approach to growth, one that is more in line with an edge mindset.

Like Gilead, the big biotechs—such as Biogen Idec, Amgen, and Genentech—tend to be much more focused than their big pharma peers. They focus on core therapeutic areas and technologies and grow their businesses through bolted-on acquisitions, not broad diversification moves. But, despite this, with revenues in the tens of billions of dollars, these companies are starting to rival big pharma in size and scale.

Gilead started out as an infectious disease company, and this largely remains its core business focus today. It built a highly successful franchise in HIV therapies.[41] When the company decided to expand, it stayed within the universe of infectious disease. In December 2002, it bought Triangle Pharmaceuticals to enter the hepatitis B market.[42] Gilead's experience in developing therapies for infectious disease helped to ensure that the success in treating HIV was replicated with hepatitis B. This leveraged its knowledge edge. It had developed a foundational asset in the infectious disease know-how and leveraged it to ensure success in transactions like the Triangle Pharmaceutical deal.

Furthermore, Gilead's know-how from a regulatory perspective (how to construct and interpret infectious disease clinical trials) and the knowledge it built regarding how to produce combination therapies for HIV all proved critical to its success in bolted-on expansions.[43] Gilead even developed an effective tiered-pricing model (which enabled its HIV products to be sold globally) that it was able to leverage for its other infectious disease therapies.[44] Its biggest transaction to date, acquiring Pharmasset in 2011 for $11 billion, enabled it to take the lead in hepatitis C therapy, a move that is expected to deliver an incremental $20 billion in revenue.[45] By any standards, this move is a major success for Gilead, a transformation to its business. Yes, this was done while remaining on the edge of its core. Its know-how and expertise in infectious disease and hepatitis gave it an advantage in seeing the potential of Pharmasset and in bringing its therapy to market. Coincidentally, around the same time, big pharma companies were beginning the process of jettisoning many of their failed diversification assets.

Why is Gilead's growth strategy consistent with an edge approach? While some of the earlier examples we have covered leveraged the product and journey aspects of edge strategy to support successful deals, Gilead's edge strategy is focused on its enterprise edge. The company leveraged its knowledge and expertise to ensure success in its transactions. Its underlying growth strategies were predicated on this. Just like Major League

Baseball, which, as discussed in chapter 4, realized that its technology for streaming online content wasn't uniquely valuable to baseball and could be leveraged to support other sports- and nonsports-related media, so too did Gilead realize that all it had learned and developed for HIV therapy development wasn't uniquely valuable to that disease. It was empowered to take on other infectious diseases like hepatitis—and win.

Seed Capital: Initiating Edges with M&A

If M&A is a tool for strategy and edge strategy is a path to growth, then we must come full circle and ask ourselves, "Does M&A have a role in edge strategy?" Our experience is that this is indeed the case. When looking at how to take advantage of an identified product or journey edge opportunity, an important option that you must not ignore is whether a small acquisition can be used to jump-start your strategic move.

Take, for example, how Best Buy seeded its journey edge strategy with an acquisition. Geek Squad was founded in 1994 by Robert Stephens, the firm's self-styled "chief inspector."[46] As personal computers became more popular in the 1990s, Stephens found a niche business in technical support and repair of the machines. By 2002, when Best Buy acquired his company, there were sixty employees that generated $3 million of annual revenues.[47]

For Best Buy, the small acquisition solved a particular problem. Store managers noticed that customers who had bought a computer from the store were starting to return with requests for help getting the computer started; in those days, the start-up manual often ran several hundred pages and was full of technical jargon. Typically, customers would go to the in-store help desk, where Best Buy associates would do their best to troubleshoot.[48]

The trouble was, more and more people started to do this. Concerned about rising customer dissatisfaction, as well as the rising cost of handling the requests, Best Buy's executives found the solution with

Geek Squad.[49] It provided a paid professional help service that could accomplish a product edge, upselling trifecta for "convenience," "relief," and "peace of mind" customer needs.

Gradually, Best Buy's managers realized that Geek Squad could help with the full range of consumer electronics goods sold across its stores, because no longer was it only computers that were difficult to get working. As Brian Dunn, president of Best Buy's retail operation, once put it: "As our products become more complex and more connected to each other, consumers are shifting from 'do-it-yourselfers' to 'do it for me.'"[50] Jeff Severts, vice president of Best Buy's services division, agreed: "Anybody can sell [you] a TV or a computer or a cellphone. The real value is in finding someone who can get this stuff to work for you and can keep it working."[51]

As Geek Squad proved to be a success, it attracted further investment. By 2010, Best Buy employed twenty-four thousand Geek Squad agents.[52] There is also a major central service depot known as "Geek Squad City."[53]

A $3 million company has grown to a $3 billion journey edge business for Best Buy.[54] In addition, analysts estimate that it enjoys a profit margin of more than 40 percent, compared to less than 5 percent in the business overall. Furthermore, Best Buy now enjoys an enhanced relationship with customers.[55]

As the company has continued to evolve its retail model, its focus on the journey edge has remained. In one of his first comments after becoming chief executive of Best Buy in 2012, Hubert Joly said, "We believe that price-competitiveness is table stakes. The way we want to win is around advice, convenience, and service."[56]

Diversification as a Risky Rationale

Diversification is a popular strategic rationale for transactions, as seen in the strategies of big pharma and ICI that we discuss in this chapter. It seems somehow at odds with everything that makes edge strategy work. We do not argue that diversification is a unilaterally bad idea. There are, in fact, examples of companies acquiring their way to diversified success; Johnson & Johnson has proven highly effective at doing this in the health-care space.[57] However, we recognize that this is a risky strategy and often fails. Moves like these have a hard time creating synergies to support the cost of a deal and also struggle to leverage existing assets and capabilities to facilitate integration.

As to whether we recommend exploring diversification strategies, we tend to adhere to the school of thought that diversification should be left to the domain of investors and that management teams should instead focus on maximizing the growth of their existing businesses, either organically or inorganically.

Practitioner's Notes

- Corporate transactions are both commonplace and exceedingly difficult to execute. However, we believe that edge strategy can help guide success in mergers and acquisitions.

- M&A is not a strategy by itself; rather, it is a valuable strategic tool to deploy in executing a larger strategy of growth. An astute manager will frame potential acquisitions as part of an edge strategy. Where she fails to see strategic value, she should be wary of the potential for an acquisition without an underlying strategic direction.

- The majority of M&A deals do, indeed, fail to generate shareholder value. Many reasons cause this failure, one of which is misinterpreting the potential for revenue synergies. Edge strategy is a valuable discipline for identifying, understanding, and derisking these important cash flows.

- The edge strategy framework is applicable at all stages of the deal life cycle, ranging from sourcing to screening and synergy valuation:

- Product edge strategies focus on how two companies' offerings can be combined to create the enhancement and upselling opportunities. Procter & Gamble's acquisition of Gillette and the roll-up transactions of NAVEX offer examples of how the acquirer's and target's product catalogs were successfully merged together to create product edge opportunities.

- Journey edge strategies point to partnerships where the company can seek and be granted permission to extend its participation in the customer's journey. By recognizing an unmet customer need for convenient and effective technical support, Best Buy's timely acquisition of the start-up Geek Squad allowed the retailer to redefine its role in the customer journey and laid the groundwork for a long-term transition into a services-focused company. In contrast, eBay's purchase of Skype offers a glimpse of a journey-based acquisition that failed several key edge tests.

- Enterprise edge strategies often require the most outside-the-box thinking, but can yield startling returns. By creating a careful inventory of the acquirer's and target's foundational assets and submitting each to the test of identifying alternate users in new business contexts, a company can begin to identify enterprise edge opportunities. Gilead's inorganic growth strategy (especially when contrasted to its acquisition-heavy cousins in big pharma) provides a compelling example of a company that has integrated an enterprise edge mindset into its deal function.

• In summary, an edge mindset can be applied to acquisitions of all sizes—large and small—and should provide a valuable perspective in any deal situation. The story of big pharma's acquisition spree provides a cautionary tale—one heeded by biotech companies like Gilead Sciences—against an undisciplined inorganic growth strategy. In contrast, Best Buy's modest purchase of a $3 million company called Geek Squad, while small at the time, has had a transformative impact on the giant retailer. What is absolutely critical in all of these situations, regardless of the size and budget of your deal team, is that you carefully identify the edge opportunities the deal will create and validate that these opportunities will, in fact, bear fruit.

CHAPTER 10

FINDING YOUR EDGE

A Ten-Step Guide

Throughout this book, we have shared a broad range of valuable and interesting observations about how companies can find profitable growth opportunities. More importantly, we hope to have also instilled in you an *edge mindset*.

The preceding chapters were a practice of sorts, helping you develop pattern recognition for the edge strategy framework. We hope that you are already thinking about the edges you encounter in your own world and that somewhere in these pages you have had moments of epiphany and recognized something familiar and applicable to your business.

Your Edge Mindset

Companies worldwide are trying to grow by making risky and bold moves. Often these moves overlook the near-field potential on the edge of a business. With an edge mindset and the edge strategy framework, you should now be able to explore this transition space and find opportunity in the borderlands between your core business and the markets beyond. You should take comfort that this approach is not novel; we did not invent edges. Our research shows that edges are present in virtually every industry. Managers and leaders have applied exactly this kind of thinking for decades, if not since the dawn of commercial activity.

You will also recognize that despite its apparent ubiquity, most companies across most industries vastly underexploit edge strategy. They rarely tap its full potential. Our research indicates that fewer than 10 percent of companies appear to make a disciplined effort to unlock edgelike opportunities.[1] Fewer still are likely conscious of what they are ignoring.

You will have seen in the many examples we detailed that, in deploying edge strategy, a company can access new sources of profitable growth that are less risky and typically higher margin than options in the core or beyond. These companies often have also made their customers happier by more completely meeting their needs or moving closer toward the completion of their missions. They have also been able to sustain the benefits of their innovation longer, as their own competitors adopt the strategies and help redefine market expectations.

With your new edge mindset, you will be thinking about what defines the edge of your current product: What could exist on the outside edge, given your customer set? What about opportunities to unbundle or de-content your offering on the inside edge? If you have subsets of customers that you think are not fully satisfied or perhaps are unprofitable, then you should be homing in on these opportunities to deploy a product edge strategy. You should also be thinking about your customers in the context of the journey that they are on, and what happens beyond your current interactions with them. What opportunities exist for you to assist them in completing more of their journey with you?

You should also be thinking about what constitutes the foundational assets that support your company's core offerings. How could these support any of the three types of edge strategy: product, journey, or perhaps even enterprise? Which are the tangible assets you deploy, and what intangible or unconstrained assets do you possess or produce? Does your company produce by-products or could you consider something produced within the context of a by-product? Take a second look at any waste stream and intangibles like data and information. As we have seen throughout this book, companies of all kinds have found ways to leverage just such assets and resources to capitalize on edge opportunities and enterprise edges in particular. You should have started to think of answers to the question, *Who, besides a direct competitor, would pay for the rights to any of my company's foundational assets?*

In all likelihood, your organization faces some similar themes to those addressed in part 2 of this book, in which we considered some of the common applications of edge strategy.

In chapter 5, we saw how product and journey edges are highly effective tools for supporting pricing strategy. Opportunities to introduce à la carte upsell offers to some or all of your customers may have occurred to you. You may have spotted how you could offer enhanced convenience or comfort to some of your customers, as in the JetBlue example. Maybe offering relief or peace-of-mind upsell strategies, as we saw used by the telecoms and automobile dealers, could resonate with the permission sets of your customers. Maybe you are in an industry where the type of passion upsell that Cirque du Soleil employed would be compelling, or one where a knowledge upsell strategy like the one Nielsen used would be valuable to customers.

Your market may be one of the many in which margin pressure is acute, and the strategies explored in chapter 6 resonate. You may acknowledge that you have unprofitable customers and are considering whether you, like W.W. Grainger, can also employ moves to unbundle some elements of your offering. This approach will challenge your unprofitable customers to either choose to alter their behavior and so reduce the cost burden they cause, or choose to pay extra for those services they valued but took for granted before. You may have recognized an opportunity to do less of something in your current core, similar to the self-service strategies retailers are starting to employ.

Similarly, if your organization is fighting the threat of commoditization, the discussions in chapter 7 prompted you to start contemplating edge-based moves to approximate customization, offer solutions, or even create targeted, recalibrated bundles. More than one of these approaches may make sense to you, and so you are considering how edge merchandising, a concerted system of coordinating these moves and evolving them, should be part of your strategy.

In addition, you may have more opportunistic thoughts on how your new edge mindset can help. One of the areas where you will want to focus your edge thinking in order to find new opportunities for growth is the data and information your company generates and uses. As we explained in chapter 8, this is one of the nascent and least exploited uses of edge strategy. Our discussion should have prompted you to start thinking about how your data could be useful to others and how it is not unilaterally useful for the purposes of your core business. You should be considering how data could form part of a product edge upsell to current customers or possibly the basis of an enterprise edge if that data, harvested and deployed differently, nearly enables a new offering with a new set of customers.

If your company is contemplating inorganic growth opportunities or even regularly executes such moves, then the application of edge thinking described in chapter 9 will have been valuable. After reading this book, you should look at possible transactions with a newfound lens. Your new edge mindset will focus you on where a deal is truly complementary and will realistically create synergies. It should help you provide greater discipline in screening for new possible deals and a framework for how to ensure that you do not overpay if you decide to proceed with an opportunity. Your new edge mindset should help you and your company beat the odds in M&A.

Overall, we hope you, like us, conclude that most companies should be able to find and successfully realize new incremental sources of profitable growth by leveraging their foundational assets more than they might have previously thought possible. We hope you are asking yourself the many questions this book poses, and that this activity sparks many new ideas for how you can find your own opportunities. Most of all, we hope you are asking the question, What is my edge strategy?

Edge Strategy in Application

Even if you fully embrace an edge mindset and the associated edge strategy framework, you still need to make it all happen. So in this final chapter, we provide a methodical process, using tools you or others in your organization already know, to put edge strategy into action.

At a high level, developing and executing growth strategies can involve some familiar steps, whether you are developing a new product, building a line extension, commercializing a new technology, or trying to launch a product in a new market. In working with many companies, industries, and geographies, we have found certain specific patterns of activities across initiatives that are especially helpful for unleashing edge economics. What we will detail here, therefore, is twofold. First, we will lay out all the steps required to apply edge strategy successfully. Second, we will detail where edge strategies require specific attention or deviate from standard ways of executing on growth strategy initiatives.

To be comprehensive, we have also mapped out these steps on the premise of a company seeking to equally explore, identify, and capitalize on any one of the three types of edge strategy. We recognize that this exhaustive approach will not always be necessary. If, by contrast, only a specific type of edge strategy is the initial focus, some of these steps are less important, as we will explain.

We generally advocate that the overall process encompasses ten steps, taking you from strategy development to activation.

- *Developing your strategy.* In these first five steps, you apply your newly honed mindset to find edge opportunities within your business.

  - *Step 1: Understand your customers.*

  - *Step 2: Fractionate your products and services.*

  - *Step 3: Map the customer journey.*

  - *Step 4: Assess your foundational assets.*

  - *Step 5: Prioritize your edge opportunities.*

- *Building the plan.* No strategy can be successful if you underinvest in detailed analytical planning; this is especially true for edge strategy. The next three steps ensure that you build the investment support needed.

  - *Step 6: Determine your likely customer adoption rates.*

  - *Step 7: Define the operating model.*

  - *Step 8: Build a winning business case.*

- *Activating the strategy.* Making strategy deliver intended results requires a balance of two things: adherence to project management principles and responding to challenges in a way that adapts to the facts on the ground, while maintaining your initial strategic direction. The final two steps help ensure successful realization of your strategic goals.

  - *Step 9: Execute the plan.*

  - *Step 10: Observe and refine.*

Developing Your Strategy

STEP 1: UNDERSTAND YOUR CUSTOMERS

Product and journey edge strategies are focused on your current customers, so an essential starting point is to understand these key stakeholders. We recommend an edge-specific needs-based segmentation for this purpose. In various ways, ask your customers why, and for what purpose, they buy your products. You want to explore what they are missing, what else they do on their journey, and where gaps are in your offer. You can then couple this with data on their characteristics and behaviors to match what they say with what they do. With this information, you will be able to assign each customer to one of a discrete set of groups or edge-specific segments.

As familiar as a company may be with its customers and its market, it needs to invest in targeted primary market research for edge strategy development to build the necessary peripheral-vision insights. Many companies perform detailed customer segmentations as part of other efforts. But we've found that using these segmentations is often inappropriate for edge strategy development. Segmentations are only useful if they are well calibrated with their purposes; for this reason, successful organizations often apply several different ones. For example, we often see executives who are tempted to use a segmentation that they use regularly for marketing communications (e-mails, direct mailings, and so on). Even if well-thought-out, descriptive, and perfectly geared toward the needs of the marketing communication group, this segmentation is unlikely to tell them much about how customers would respond to edge products. Existing segmentations tend to be focused on selling core product. If you don't take the time and effort to analyze edge receptivity empirically at the start, then your strategy will be unlikely to have the analytical backbone it needs to gain approval later.

You and your research team will also want to carefully reflect on new edge-based segments: Who are each of these customers? What do they value most in your offer? What unmet needs do they have? For example, would certain customers appreciate the extra peace of mind that comes with an extended warranty? Do others require special assistance in installing, maintaining, or servicing your product? Are there customers who do not value certain aspects of your core offer?

These segments reflect how each group engages with your offer. Therefore, this kind of segmentation analysis enables you to understand which variations of customer needs have sufficient traction to support a viable edge business case.

STEP 2: FRACTIONATE YOUR PRODUCTS AND SERVICES

Central to any edge strategy is an understanding of what you currently do. In returning to the framework from the first part of this book, the second step involves carefully defining your core offering to juxtapose it with the customer permission set.

Begin by "fractionating" your offering, that is, conducting a detailed analysis of each service or product you offer. By doing this, you will understand the component parts of your offer and how each fulfills different types of customer needs. Take your customer's perspective during this process. How does your customer see your product or service? Repeat this thought process for each product or service and for each customer segment defined in step one.

For example, consider a company that manufactures industrial etching tools. It offers a set of service levels depending on the customer type (for instance, large multinational customers have a dedicated account manager and twenty-four-hour technical support; smaller customers make purchases via distributors and have online support and a nine-to-five telephone help line). These different service levels are fractions or elements of the offer each customer segment receives. Rigorously cataloging the elements of the offer by customer segment is what we call "fractionating." Each of these discrete elements could form the basis of either edge-based upselling or, potentially, unbundling strategies.

The easiest and most direct way to fractionate is to speak to your customers and your frontline sales employees. How do they define your offer? What basic customer needs are you meeting? What problems are you solving? By adopting this needs-focused view, you can build a valuable perspective on how your offer is currently configured and how it could alternatively be fractionated.

STEP 3: MAP THE CUSTOMER JOURNEY

Needs-based segmentation and product fractionation are great starting points. However, taken alone, they would miss the possibility of journey edge opportunities. If you consider your customers only on the basis of the transactions you have with them today, you can miss their underlying agenda. You must also investigate how your product or service fits into their journeys.

As we described in chapter 3, the key is to first recognize the mission your customers are trying to complete and, for a given segment, the different missions they have. For each mission, you need therefore to understand the holistic journey your customer is on in order to complete it and break that journey into discrete elements. Then you must consider the customer's specific needs at each stage of the journey.

When building this view, it is important to adopt the customer's perspective and engage him in conversations about how your business solves his underlying needs. You need to specifically emphasize the stages immediately before and after she engages your product or service, where a journey edge is most likely. This significant task must be mapped for each identified customer segment.

In some cases, we have found that simply talking through the journey with customers in a focus group setting can yield valuable insights. Again, do this discretely for each customer segment. In other cases, it's necessary to go out and mimic the customer experience yourself. Consider walking through the journey with some actual customers, observing

Lessons Learned: Multiple Journeys, Same Customer

If you're a pet owner, you know that the pet supply business can be a highly competitive market. You can purchase food, toys, treats, and even veterinary medicine from a number of different types of stores—big-box retailers, pet specialty retailers, local grooming studios, and even online retailers like Amazon. How could a pet supply retailer find an edge strategy in this crowded market? If you consider the customer journeys for this business, you would recognize that they are highly differentiated based on two different factors: the type of product the customer is shopping for and the age of her pet. For example, puppy owners looking for training toys often prefer a high-touch, *knowledge-based* sales process and tend to ask the sales associates a lot of questions. On the other hand, when the same puppy owners are shopping for dog food, they tend to view it as a *convenience-driven* purchase; they are looking to "get in, get out" because they know what they want.

This is a simple but significant insight. Even within a single customer segment (the puppy owner), there might be multiple journeys based on the context of the purchase. If a pet retailer were to plot out a single mega-journey, encompassing every significant step along the way for all customer types, missions, and products, it would miss important insights about the convenience-driven nature of some purchases and the knowledge requirements of others. As detailed in chapter 5, these two insights guide you to different types of product edge strategy.

---

them as they engage with your offering. While you may do this regularly in the context of your current offer, for identifying edges, take the extra steps to join their journey earlier and stay with them longer, after they have moved on from your current offer. What brought them to the purchase point? What key steps did they take to get there? What will they do next, immediately after they disengage from the business? What is the final resting place of the purchase—be it a TV installed and fully wired to your surround-sound system, or a more efficient warehousing operation as a result of a third-party logistics service.

STEP 4: ASSESS YOUR FOUNDATIONAL ASSETS

As detailed in chapter 1, all edge strategies are supported by leveraging the latent value in the existing foundational assets of a company. We therefore recommend a regimented process of working through your company's resources and capabilities.

First, develop an inventory of all your assets. This assessment may seem simple, but it is important to consider all possible forms of asset, not only hard assets like equipment and facilities, but also capabilities like customer service expertise and empowered leadership culture. Also consider your softer assets—knowledge, technology, information and data, and expertise in a specific topic. Channel access and market presence are also good examples of market-based assets that companies can leverage. We encourage you to be as broad in your consideration as possible.

With a comprehensive list of foundational assets in hand, work through a simple checklist to consider how the different assets can provide a foundation for your edge strategy:

- What precisely is the value of this asset to my current customers?

- Is the use of this asset uniquely aligned to meeting these needs?

- How could the asset be employed to support my customer beyond the current purpose?

Steps one through three are mainly focused on finding product and journey edges through an examination of your customers and their needs and missions; this is an outside view of edge opportunities. The additional lens of exploring the utility of foundational assets and asking how they can be leveraged for moves along product and journey edges brings together the inside view and completes this thinking. With both perspectives in hand, you can examine where opportunities are complementary: where an identified use of your assets aligns with a recognized unmet need of a customer segment. You can do this exercise effectively in one or more internal workshops of commercial and operational managers. Moderation and leadership are important in any such activity, and a dedicated owner of the edge strategy initiative should prepare structured materials, lead the session, and capture takeaways.

Testing for Enterprise Edges

In order to identify opportunities for moves along enterprise edges, you must take this assessment a step deeper. We recommend asking some additional questions:

- Do you have underutilized physical assets?

- Does your production process create by-products that you are not fully monetizing?

- Are any of your assets unconstrained or intangible?

- Would any companies, other than a competitor, value any aspect of your business?

- If so, can you provide them access without affecting your core business?

- How are those companies currently satisfying that need?

- Can your company offer them a better solution?

- Is there a reasonable path to market with those customers?

When exploring assets in pursuit of an enterprise edge, employ a similar workshop approach, but augment this discussion with an expert panel. Select a diverse group of industry executives and observers from other related markets in the sphere of influence affected by your business. Then, stage a facilitated workshop at which you ask the experts to explain where your assets could be valuable beyond your current market. Sometimes we invite executives from customers or suppliers, as well as key industry observers in sectors further afield from our client's, but with the potential to find value; academics are often a valuable addition to these sessions. This activity is highly valuable; an external view can help your team focus on the periphery of your business and take a perpendicular view of its assets and capabilities.

STEP 5: PRIORITIZE YOUR EDGE OPPORTUNITIES

After completing the first four steps, you may have discovered a potentially long list of product, journey, and enterprise edge "proto" opportunities. The next step is to sort through them and create a short list of the most promising ones, using a methodical, objective approach.

Begin by establishing defined, edge-specific criteria consistent with your company's existing strategic goals. These measurable criteria will typically include the profit potential of the opportunity, the feasibility of implementation, the amount of investment, the degree of risk, the time to delivery, and so on.

Make sure that you have sufficient information to evaluate the opportunities along each dimension. Typically, the types of information you need will not be readily available or quantified. To overcome this, identify a few key functional experts in your organization with whom you work one-on-one to assemble high-level "what you need to believe" business cases for each opportunity. You can then compare and prioritize these in a workshop with a cross-section of your organizational stakeholders (for example, sales, marketing, finance, operations, technology, human resources).

Next, have a steering team of senior leaders review the opportunities and the prioritized list of the best opportunities to decide which merit further consideration and investment. This should set the strategic priorities to take forward into detailed planning.

Building the Plan

STEP 6: DETERMINE YOUR LIKELY CUSTOMER ADOPTION RATES

Once you have determined a short list of strategic options, you have the basis of your strategy. The next step is to build the detailed plan that will define not only what is needed to realize the strategy but also what outcomes to expect. You may still have a short list of options; if so, this helps to maintain flexibility. At this stage, you cannot fully know which will be the true winners or where hidden red-flag issues exist, so try to move more than a single idea into detailed planning. This way, if issues emerge with one idea, you can pivot your focus to the remaining option(s) without going back to the drawing board.

Predicting the revenue potential of any edge strategy, regardless of whether it is product, journey, or enterprise, is a key effort that involves deep quantitative research with your customers (or, in the case of many enterprise edges, customers in a new market). First, understand how many of your customers will buy the edge offering. What will be the adoption rate? How many of your customers will purchase the new à la carte feature? What percent of your customer base would purchase the new services? Intimately linked with this question is the price of the offering. As such, test how customers react to various prices. Edge strategy uses marginal economics, and pricing can therefore be set to maximize profitability.

One tool for building robust business cases for edge strategy is choice-based conjoint analysis. At its simplest level, conjoint analysis involves surveying or interviewing customers and asking them to choose between different versions of a complete solution. This method is ideal for product and journey edge strategy testing as the approach allows you to toggle in and out various levels of edge elements. For example, a car manufacturer might ask customers to choose between a sedan with standard seats and an XM radio for $25,000, or the same base model with leather seats, a DVD player, and navigation system for $30,000. While this may seem like an arbitrary question, the key with conjoint analysis is to repeat it for many possible product combinations and customers. Once you have explored all possible product combinations tested over a variety of price points, you can then employ statistical analysis software to work out the value of each edge element or attribute. In other words, over a large enough number of responses, this type of study allows you to understand, on a quantifiable basis, how customers value the different edge elements in your offering and what price they are willing to pay for them.

With this knowledge, you can then vary the price of your edge offerings in order to reach the adoption rates that should maximize profitability.

STEP 7: DEFINE THE OPERATING MODEL

The next step is to address the basic question of how to deliver this strategy. Developing an understanding of the required operating model is a key step to answering four essential questions for any edge business case:

1. What operating costs are required to enable your edge opportunity?

2. What investment will you need?

3. What changes to your organization will you need to make?

4. What is the timeline for launching the product?

First, define the manifestation of each edge product, that is, how will customers experience it, where, and in what way? To do this, develop a detailed product profile or specification that fully defines what you want this product to be and how customers will experience it. Often, this road map explains how the customer will experience the product at launch and then how you will expand it in the future. For example, in a launch, specification pricing may be fixed, but you might contemplate moving to a dynamic pricing model in the future. You might launch with only one point of sale but plan to expand to several in the future.

Next, examine how the organization needs to change in order to activate this new product experience. A great framework for this step is to adhere to the hierarchy of "people, process, technology."

Begin with the *people*. Who in your organization will be involved in offering and fulfilling the edge strategy? How will their roles be affected? Will you need to create new roles? How will you design responsibilities and ownership for the new edge products? This will help to inform the labor cost impact of the new product. It also informs the requirements for implementation. Who will need to be engaged? What will they need to know and understand about the new strategy?

One of the common reasons that companies have not taken advantage of edge strategies is because there is no clear owner in the organization for these initiatives. As we will detail in step nine, edge strategy typically crosses functions, and often no single area has clear responsibility. Finding and appointing someone to own edge initiatives is often the first step to establishing real momentum. It is also essential to have a single dedicated owner once edge opportunities are in operation in order to ensure delivery of results.

Next, consider the *processes*. How will your teams' day-to-day activities need to change to ensure that they carry out the new service, product, or activity effectively? What do you need to do in order to bring this offering to your customers? For example, will you need to train employees? This stage is critical for determining the activities you will need to successfully implement the strategy, the new systems you need, the metrics you need to measure, the training and changes to operating procedures, and the likely duration of this change process.

Finally, after you have considered the first two criteria, turn to *technology*. Technology should be a function of the process requirements determined in the prior step. Avoid a scenario in which strategies become captive and overly influenced by the availability or requirements of technology.

Building this operating model requires broad organizational engagement. At this point, you should typically have a working team of cross-functional point managers from the company engaging regularly. This team must work through the implication for their own functions using the steps discussed earlier and then develop the overall model.

STEP 8: BUILD A WINNING BUSINESS CASE

A big hurdle in making edge strategy a reality is building the case for investment. Every organization has constrained resources, and edge strategy, like any other, must vie with all the other requirements and obligations for funding that a company wrestles with regularly.

A robust economic model is an essential component of a successful business case. This is where the detailed effort to quantify the revenue opportunity and map out the operating model we have discussed will bear fruit. A strong business case is one that delineates a multiyear financial view and drives this analysis to cash flow, fully considering all investment capital over time. It considers sensitivity to key inputs and tests scenarios for how a launch may materialize, given acknowledged uncertainties. It includes a fulsome risk assessment, one that has engaged a comprehensive group of functional leaders.

Decisions rarely happen in the moment, particularly for opportunities that are, by design, on the periphery of your core business. Be patient and engage in an extended period of socialization and buy-in before such investment sessions. Ideally, almost no one in attendance should be unfamiliar or disagree radically with what you present before the session. This is vital for flushing out concerns or objections ahead of time so that you can address and mitigate them.

Few organizations welcome change, and some operational executives are programmed to avoid it at all costs. This inherent challenge to corporate growth is often especially acute for edge strategies. All too often, edge strategies can be viewed as a minor benefit if only considered from a revenue context and not worth the distraction to the core. So the creation of a fully vetted business case that quantifies the bottom-line impact is essential. When initiatives are evaluated without taking the time to drive the analysis to the profit line, with functional buy-in to key cost line items, promising edge strategies can fall foul of the committee room of opinion and institutional folklore.

Activating the Strategy

STEP 9: EXECUTE THE PLAN

Once you have defined your edge strategy and the business case has been approved, you can begin the strategy activation phase. Here an edge strategy project can start to look a lot more like a typical capital project implementation or change management process. You have achieved the critical task of securing buy-in and approval. This does not mean, however, that success is assured.

An essential element of implementing edge strategies is to employ good project management practices: a dedicated strategy activation office; a seasoned project management team; sensible governance structure; clearly articulated, measurable goals and objectives; achievable timelines; project procedures; and resource management tools.

A specific challenge to be aware of in edge strategy activation, as with development, is dealing with its cross-organizational nature. Unlike many investment projects and initiatives, edge strategy does not often come from an established operating function, for example, like a manufacturing plant building a new production line. It is often a nascent activity run by a small group from, say, the marketing team or strategy group. The implementation process tends to touch many different functions: sales, procurement, IT, finance, operations, customer service, HR, communications, but none of whom will own the final result. As such, an edge strategy activation office should be established in order to foster cooperation and engagement from people across the organization for which the goals of the project may not be a day-to-day focus. The office requires a project team with particular skills in building relationships and influencing without direct authority, which is not always present in a traditional project management office function. This approach also factors in the amount of engagement and time for buy-in that should be built into the project timeline.

While activating an edge strategy—as detailed in this book—is far less risky than many growth strategy options, there is always some risk associated with poor execution: what we call "yield loss." Yield loss occurs when the final solution fails to achieve some of the original financial goals of the project, which happens most often because critical aspects of the project were compromised during activation. To mitigate this, ensure that the strategy activation office retains members of the original strategy development group. By doing this, you ensure that, as challenges arise during implementation or you discover unforeseen complexities, you develop solutions with an intimate awareness and sensitivity to the commercial underpinning of the strategy versus ones that purely prioritize expediency. This explicit inclusion of a strategy perspective throughout implementation is what distinguishes activating strategy from simply project management, and is essential to mitigating yield loss.

STEP 10: OBSERVE AND REFINE

Strategies are rarely conceived in their final form. You will inevitably adjust your strategy along the way. This is especially true with edge strategy, given the inherently incremental nature of these opportunities; it is likely that you can push the strategy further once it is launched. Building in an expectation that this will happen—and that the same level of strategic thinking will be in place to support these adjustments, as was the case in the initial development of the strategy—is critical to making the most of your edge strategy.

A structured and metrics-based monitoring and refinement effort should operate for at least the first year after the launch of your edge strategy. Are adoption rates in line with what you expected? Are there any features that are playing particularly well (or poorly) in the market? Are you hitting monthly sales milestones? Are there delivery failures or unexpected cost increases?

As part of the activation phase, the strategy activation office should create goals that will be monitored in the first twelve months after launch. You can use a dashboard that monitors the company's progress against these goals. Are sales tracking along with your expectations? Are you investing the appropriate amount of resources?

This same strategy activation office should also meet monthly post-launch to review the dashboard and correct course where necessary. During the first few months that your edge strategy is "in market," you will get invaluable feedback from customers. Could you tweak pricing to drive adoption in a key customer segment? Has the competitive response paved the way for additional edge strategies? Recall the examples of United Airlines in chapter 6, which was the first to market with checked-bag fees. But shortly after all major airlines started charging for the second checked bag, American Airlines announced it would charge for the *first* bag too. United was paying attention and was able to respond quickly by introducing a similar policy a few weeks later.

There are no silver bullets in growth strategy. Nothing is free, and there are few truly untapped market opportunities for most companies. New competitors to your core businesses emerge every day and are constantly probing, seeking to nullify points of differentiation. Your customers are empowered with information and technology to evaluate every facet of your offer and hold you constantly accountable on performance and price. The pace of competition has never been faster, and the market has never been more ruthless at exposing laggards.

Yet, there is a place you can look and a discipline you can bring that should help you unlock incremental sources of profit for your company—a way of finding growth that avoids the win-lose market share game and that is less risky and easier to realize.

We hope this book empowers you with a new, complementary mindset. We hope that it provides you with a powerful new tool to affect your company's growth potential. All that remains is for you to find your edge strategy.

NOTES

Chapter 1

1. Thomas D. Sisk and James Battin, "Habitat Edges and Avian Ecology: Geographic Patterns and Insights for Western Landscapes," *Studies in Avian Biology* 25 (2002): 30–48.

2. Eugene P. Odum and Gary W. Barrett, *Fundamentals of Ecology* (Belmont, CA: Thomson Brooks/Cole, 2005), 386.

3. Ibid.

4. "Blue Planet: Coasts," World Wildlife Federation, accessed September 29, 2014.

5. "Canada Facts," *National Geographic Atlas of the World*, 8th ed., September 2004.

6. "Table 363. U.S.-Canada and U.S.-Mexico Border Lengths," US Census Bureau: Statistical Abstract of the United States, 2012.

7. Karl Polanyi, "Ports of Trade in Early Societies," *Journal of Economic History* 23, no. 1 (March 1963): 30–45.

8. Terrel Gallaway, "Life on the Edge: A Look at Ports of Trade and Other Ecotones," *Journal of Economic Issues* 39, no. 3 (September 2005): 716.

9. Irna Qureshi, "The Grand Trunk Road: A Journey Along India's Life Line," *Sabotage Times*, June 27, 2013.

10. Ella Davies, "Lords of the Twilight Zone," BBC News, October 28, 2010.

11. "Blue Planet: Coasts," World Wildlife Federation.

12. Davies, "Lords of the Twilight Zone."

13. Every indexed company was meticulously screened for edge strategies using publicly available resources, including but not limited to company websites, SEC filings, and press releases. Each identified edge strategy was accounted for and characterized based on the definitions provided in this book. Companies demonstrating unique and exemplary utilization of edge strategies were deemed "edge achievers."

14. L.E.K. Consulting, "Analysis of Edge Strategy Prevalence," unpublished study, November 2014.

15. Ibid.

16. Ibid.

17. Ibid.

Chapter 2

1. "Apple Retail Stores Welcome Over 7700 People in First Two Days," Apple press release, May 21, 2001; and "Apple Presents iPod," Apple press release, October 23, 2001.

2. "Apple Presents iPod."

3. Ralph Graves, "iPod Generations Chart," Crutchfield New Media, http://www.crutchfield.com/S-3F2TdVQB9Rp/learn/learningcenter/MP3/iPodgenchart.html, accessed January 5, 2015.

4. This device, once connected to your iPod, would generate an FM signal broadcasting your music from the player like a tiny radio station. This would allow you to tune your car radio to this signal and play your iPod through your car. Bluetooth has largely replaced this function today.

5. "Apple Developer Program," Apple.com, accessed July 22, 2015; and "Car & Travel," Apple.com, accessed January 5, 2015.

6. "Make Sure Your Charger Is the Real Deal," GriffinTechnology.com, accessed January 5, 2015; and "Car & Travel," Apple.com.

7. iTunes was launched about nine months before the iPod and was actually the result of an acquisition of another product, SoundJam MP, in 2000. Michael Simon, "The Complete iTunes History—SoundJam MP to iTunes 9," MacLife.com, September 11, 2009.

8. According to Apple, in 2014 there were 800 million iTunes accounts (Juli Clover, "iTunes by the Numbers: 800M Accounts, $5.2B in Billings, 70B App Downloads," MacRumors.com, April 23, 2014) and net sales of $10.2 billion (Lance Whitney "Apple Reveals Drop in Sales of iTunes Music," CNET, October 28, 2014), including app downloads.

9. Neil Hughes, "Apple's App Store Revenue on Track to Surpass iTunes Store by End of This Year," *AppleInsider*, May 28, 2014.

10. Nick Wingfield, "iPhone Calls on Software Developers—Apple's App Store Will Create a Marketplace for Anyone to Sell Downloadable Games, Tools," *Wall Street Journal*, July 10, 2008.

11. Ibid.

12. Ibid.

13. "Clash of Clans," Think Gaming, accessed January 5, 2015; and Bernhard Warner, "Finland's Supercell: Mobile Games with Megaprofits," *Bloomberg Businessweek*, May 2, 2013.

14. Warner, "Finland's Supercell."

15. Ibid., and "Clash of Clans."

16. Stephanie L. Kimbro, "Law a la Carte: The Case for Unbundling Legal Services," *GP Solo* (American Bar Association) 29, no. 5 (September/October 2012): 30–34; and "Software Becomes a Product," Computer History Museum, accessed January 5, 2015.

17. Adrian Covert, "A decade of iTunes singles killed the music industry," CNN Money, April 25, 2013.

Chapter 3

1. Historical financial data from Yahoo! Finance, accessed January 6, 2015.

2. Colfax Corporation, 2014 Annual Report, 10-K filing for the period ending December 31, 2014.

3. Ibid.

4. Ibid.

5. "ESAB University," ESABNA.com, accessed January 8, 2015; "Training Programs," EsabNA.com, accessed January 8, 2015; and "Value Added Engineering," ESABNA.com, accessed January 8, 2015.

6. "Value Added Engineering," ESABNA.com.

7. "Whole Foods Market History," WholeFoodsMarket.com, accessed January 8, 2015.

8. Walter Robb, Whole Foods Market, quarterly earnings call, July 28, 2005.

9. Whole Foods Market, quarterly earnings call, February 8, 2006.

10. Walter Robb, Whole Foods Market, quarterly earnings call, November 19, 2002; and James Sud, Whole Foods Market, quarterly earnings call, July 30, 2003.

11. Whole Foods Market, 2014 Annual Report.

12. "Gross Profit Margin Data from NBJ's Natural Foods Merchandiser Survey: NBJ Data Chart 124," *Nutrition Business Journal*, August 2008; and Whole Foods Market, 2014 Annual Report.

13. Whole Foods Market, quarterly earnings call, July 28, 2005.

14. L.E.K. Consulting, "Analysis of Edge Strategy Prevalence," unpublished study, November 2014.

15. Ibid.

16. Colour Life Services Group Co., Limited, "Global Offering," Share offering prospectus, June 17, 2014.

17. Ibid.

18. Colour Life Services Group Co., Limited, "2014 Interim Result Presentation," investor presentation, August 18, 2014.

19. Colour Life Services Group Co., Limited, "Global Offering."

20. Ibid.

21. Ibid.

22. Colour Life Services Group Co., Limited, 2014 Annual Report, August 14, 2014.

23. Colour Life Services Group Co., Limited, "China's Largest Residential Community Service Operator: Annual Report FSY 2014," investor presentation, March 2015.

Chapter 4

1. "Farming the Wind: Wind Power and Agriculture," Union of Concerned Scientists, accessed October 20, 2014.

2. Ibid.

3. Ibid.

4. Jeremy Weber, Jason Brown, and John Pender, "Rural Wealth Creation and Emerging Energy Industries: Lease and Royalty Payments to Farm Households and Businesses," Federal Reserve Bank of Kansas City Research working paper, June 2013, citing Penn State University, "Natural Gas Exploration: A Landowners Guide to Financial Management," 2009; and Dwight Aakre and Ron Haugen, "Wind Turbine Lease Considerations for Landowners," North Dakota State University Extension Service, February 2010.

5. Frank Wardynski, "Feeding Corn Stalks on Dairy Farms: Lactating Cows," Michigan State University, October 23, 2012.

6. "How Refining Works" and "Chemical Products," BP.com, accessed July 22, 2015.

7. UnitedHealth Group, 2014 Annual Report.

8. Ibid.; and "Core U.S. Data Assets," Product Sheet, Optum, 2014.

9. "Independent Expert Physician Advisory Board Formed to Advance Ingenix Efforts to Modernize the Health Care Delivery System," UnitedHealth Group press release, October 26, 2010.

10. "UnitedHealth Group," PaineWebber, March 19, 1999.

11. "Claims Data: Unparalleled Assets to Support Decision Making," Optum.com, accessed July 31, 2015.

12. "Core U.S. Data Assets," Product Sheet, Optum, 2014; "Retrospective Database Analysis," Optum, 2013; "Retrospective Databases," Optum.com, accessed September 16, 2014; and "Clinformatics for Market Intelligence," Optum.com, accessed September 16, 2014.

13. "Clinformatics Data Mart," Optum.com, accessed January 5, 2015.

14. UnitedHealth Group, 2014 Annual Report; and UnitedHealth Group, 2008 Annual Report.

15. L.E.K. Consulting, "Analysis of Edge Strategy Prevalence," unpublished study, June 2015; growth rates calculated from historical company financial reports, 2006–2014.

16. UnitedHealth Group, 2014 Annual Report.

17. Adrienne So, "Your Local Beer Isn't as Local as You Think," Slate.com, August 13, 2013; "Advantages to Using a Toll Food Manufacturing Company," PacMoore.com, accessed January 6, 2015; and "Outsourcing Partner for Chemical Services," ProChem-gmbh.de, accessed January 6, 2015.

18. "Offering You Meeting Room Rentals," University of Phoenix, accessed January 6, 2015.

19. Chuck Salter, "MLB Advanced Media's Bob Bowman is Playing Digital Hardball. And He's Winning," *Fast Company*, March 19, 2012; and Ted Berg, "The Incredibly Simple Way to Stop MLB's Increasing Length of Games," *USA Today Sports*, July 18, 2014.

20. Anita Elberse, "Major League Baseball Advanced Media: America's Pastime Goes Digital," Case 510-092 (Boston: Harvard Business School, 2011).

21. Ibid.

22. Ibid.

23. Ibid.

24. Salter, "MLB Advanced Media's Bob Bowman Is Playing Digital Hardball."

25. Elberse, "Major League Baseball Advanced Media: America's Pastime Goes Digital."

26. Brad Stone, "Major League Baseball to Stream ESPN Events," *New York Times*, March 8, 2010.

27. Elberse, "Major League Baseball Advanced Media: America's Pastime Goes Digital."

28. Ira Broadway, "How Major League Baseball Helps ESPN Stream World Cup Soccer," *Bloomberg Businessweek*, June 5, 2014.

29. Ibid.; and "Guns N' Roses Announce 'Chinese Democracy' North American Tour and Strategic Relationship with Major League Baseball Advanced Media," PR Newswire, September 29, 2006.

30. Salter, "MLB Advanced Media's Bob Bowman Is Playing Digital Hardball."

31. Elberse, "Major League Baseball Advanced Media: America's Pastime Goes Digital"; and Broadway, "How Major League Baseball Helps ESPN Stream World Cup Soccer."

32. Robert Huckman, "Amazon Web Services," Case 609-048 (Boston: Harvard Business School, 2012).

33. Ibid.

34. Greg Bensinger, "Boss Talk: Meet the Man Who Really Runs the Internet," *Wall Street Journal*, November 12, 2013.

35. Quentin Hardy, "Active in Cloud, Amazon Reshapes Computing," *New York Times*, August 27, 2012.

36. Huckman, "Amazon Web Services."

37. Ibid.

38. Ibid.

39. Ibid.

40. Barb Darrow, "Amazon Web Services Is a $5 Billion Business—and Growing Fast," Fortune.com, April 23, 2015.

41. Huckman, "Amazon Web Services"; and Larry Dingan, "Amazon Posts Its First Net Profit," CNET News, January 22, 2002.

42. Hardy, "Active in Cloud, Amazon Reshapes Computing."

43. Huckman, "Amazon Web Services."

44. Bensinger, "Boss Talk: Meet the Man Who Really Runs the Internet."

Chapter 5

1. Andrew Rees, "Take a Stand Against Margin Pressure," *L.E.K. Consulting Executive Insights* VII, no. 1 (2005): 1–6.

2. L.E.K. Consulting, "Analysis of Edge Strategy Prevalence," unpublished study, November 2014.

3. Historical annual reports for Carnival, Norwegian, and Royal Caribbean cruise lines, 1996–2014; and "Financial Breakdown of Typical Cruiser," Cruise Market Watch, accessed August 20, 2014.

4. John A. Quelch and Margaret L. Rodriguez, "Royal Caribbean Cruises Ltd.: Safety, Environment, and Health," Case 514-069 (Boston: Harvard Business School, 2014), 1; and Jennifer Eblin, "Royal Caribbean Cruises History," *USA Today*, accessed August 25, 2014.

5. "About Royal Caribbean," Royal Caribbean International, accessed August 25, 2014; Allan E. Jordan, "The Transnationals," *Cruise Travel*, February 2009; and "Case Studies—Cruise Ship: Royal Caribbean International," WaveLoch.com, accessed January 7, 2015.

6. Lynda M. Applegate, Robert J. Kwortnik, and Gabriele Piccoli, "Carnival Cruise Lines," Case 806-015 (Boston: Harvard Business School, 2006), 3; and "About Royal Caribbean," Royal Caribbean International.

7. "Allure of the Seas," Royal Caribbean International, accessed December 18, 2014; and Michael Taylor and Ken Mark, "Oasis of the Seas: The Largest Cruise Liner in the World" (London, Ontario: Richard Ivey School of Business, 2011), 3.

8. Quelch and Rodriguez, "Royal Caribbean Cruises Ltd.: Safety, Environment, and Health," 16; and "Allure of the Seas," Royal Caribbean International.

9. "Allure of the Seas," Royal Caribbean International.

10. "RCL Ticket Prices," Royal Caribbean International, accessed December 18, 2014.

11. "Large Stateroom," Royal Caribbean International, accessed December 18, 2014.

12. "Beverage Packages," Royal Caribbean International, accessed December 18, 2014.

13. "Allure of the Seas," Royal Caribbean International.

14. Park West Gallery, "Art Auctions," accessed July 31, 2015.

15. "Allure of the Seas," Royal Caribbean International.

16. Hertz, press release, July 27, 2015.

17. Mark Clothier, "Hertz Seen Taking $200 Million Writedown on Aging Fleet," *Bloomberg News*, September 10, 2014; and Auto Rental News "2014 U.S. Car Rental Market: Fleet, Locations and Revenue," Fact Book 2015

18. Enterprise Holdings, press release, May 23, 2014; and Charisse Jones, "Rental Cars: Is It Worth It to Prepay for Gas?" *USA Today*, May 21, 2013.

19. "Fuel Purchase Option," Hertz.com, accessed December 22, 2014.

20. Southwest Airlines, 2014 Annual Report; and JetBlue, 2014 Annual Report.

21. Elliott N. Weiss and Marlene Friesen, "The JetBlue Story" (Charlottesville: University of Virginia, 2005).

22. Charisse Jones, "JetBlue Launches Premium Brand called Mint," *USA Today*, September 30, 2013.

23. JetBlue earnings conference call, January 30, 2007.

24. "Even More Legroom Announced by JetBlue Airways," *Airline Industry Information*, March 20, 2008.

25. Mary Schlangenstein, "JetBlue Removing Seats to Cut Costs," *Desert News*, December 15, 2006.

26. "Even More Legroom Announced by JetBlue Airways," *Airline Industry Information*.

27. JetBlue, press release, March 19, 2008.

28. JetBlue, 2011 Annual Report.

29. "Optional Services and Fees," JetBlue.com, accessed December 22, 2014.

30. Jack Nicas, "JetBlue to Add Bag Fees, Cut Legroom," *Wall Street Journal*, November 20, 2014.

31. Anita Taff, "FCC May Be Referee in Caller ID Dispute," *Network Journal* 7, no. 7 (September 10, 1990): 13–14; and Daniel J.Wakin, "New Jersey Bell Wins Approval for Controversial Call Identification Feature," Associated Press, September 18, 1987.

32. "'Caller ID' Stirs Debate on Phone Privacy," *New York Times*, February 11, 1990.

33. David Jacobson, "Call ID Service Makes Science Fiction a Reality," *Los Angeles Times*, January 21, 1990.

34. Wayne King, "Our Towns: Number, Please: Adieu Anonymity on the Telephone," *New York Times*, April 14, 1989.

35. Duane Stoltzfus, "Caller ID on the Line: Lifesaver, or Invasion of Privacy?" *The Record* (New Jersey), August 17, 1992.

36. Ted Duncombe, "'Caller ID' Draws Static from Consumer, Rights Advocates," Associated Press, March 10, 1989.

37. Kathleen O'Brien, "No More Mystery Phone Calls," *The Record* (New Jersey), October 13, 1988.

38. L.E.K. Consulting, "Analysis of Edge Strategy Prevalence."

39. Jim Henry, "Ding-and-Dent Products Gain from Leasing, Bundling," *Automotive News*, June 11, 2014.

40. Asbury Automotive Group, 2014 Annual Report.

41. "Dealer Insights," Eisner Amper, July/August 2014.

42. NADA DATA: State of the Industry Report, 2014.

43. Jim Leman, "The Critical Role of Today's F&I Department," *Dealer Marketing*, accessed September 8, 2014.

44. Mac Gordon, "Auto Dealers Rely on F&I," *First Innovations*, 2011.

45. Asbury Automotive Group, 2014 Annual Report.

46. Ramon Casadesus-Masanell and Maxime Aucoin, "Cirque du Soleil— The High-Wire Act of Building Sustainable Partnerships," Case 709-411 (Boston: Harvard Business School, 2010).

47. "LOVE: Insider Access VIP Tickets," Showtickets.com, accessed December 22, 2014.

48. Ann Shields, "Unitard Not Required: Go Backstage at Cirque du Soleil," *Travel and Leisure*, March 24, 2011.

49. "LOVE: Insider Access VIP Tickets," Showtickets.com.

50. Casadesus-Masanell and Aucoin, "Cirque du Soleil."

51. Ibid.; and Mark MacKinnon, "Inside the Kremlin Walls, Canada's Circus Spectacular Finds a Blueprint for Growth," *Globe and Mail*, March 24, 2012.

52. "Apple Retail Store—Workshops," Apple.com, accessed December 22, 2014.

53. "Apple Retail Store—One to One," Apple.com, accessed December 22, 2014.

54. "Careers," Nielsen.com, accessed December 22, 2014.

55. "Retail Measurement," Nielsen.com, accessed December 22, 2014.

56. "Solutions," Nielsen.com, accessed December 22, 2014.

57. L.E.K. Consulting, "Analysis of Edge Strategy Prevalence."

Chapter 6

1. W.W. Grainger, 2014 Annual Report.

2. L.E.K. Consulting, "Analysis of Edge Strategy Prevalence," unpublished study, November 2014.

3. Ibid.

4. Fred L. Smith and Braden Cox, "Airline Deregulation," Library of Economics and Liberty, accessed December 23, 2014.

5. Alan Lewis and Dan McKone, "How the U.S. Airline Industry Found Its Edge," *Harvard Business Review,* September 26, 2013.

6. L.E.K. Consulting, "Analysis of Edge Strategy Prevalence"; and Morningstar historical market capitalizations for Southwest Airlines, United Continental, Delta Air Lines, and American Airlines.

7. "The Runway to the Final Four," CNN Money, accessed September 3, 2014.

8. L.E.K. Consulting, "Analysis of Edge Strategy Prevalence."

9. "Crude Oil (Petroleum); Dated Brent Daily Price," IndexMundi, accessed September 3, 2014.

10. United Airlines historical financials for the period 2006–2009 from UAL Corporation, 2008 Annual Report and 2009 Annual Report.

11. Ibid.

12. "UAL 2013 Investor Day Presentation," United Airlines, November 19, 2013; and United Airlines historical financials for the period 2006–2009 from UAL Corporation, 2008 Annual Report and 2009 Annual Report.

13. "Crude Oil (Petroleum); Dated Brent Daily Price," IndexMundi; and "United Airlines Announces New Checked Bag Policy," Dow Jones News Service, February 4, 2008.

14. Joe Sharkey, "United Adds a Checked-Bag Fee," *New York Times,* February 5, 2008.

15. Chris Kahn, "US Airways Cuts Free Baggage Allowance to 1 Checked-in Suitcase," AP Newswires, February 26, 2008; "Delta Also to Charge $25 for Second Checked Bag," *Times Union,* March 25, 2008; "American Air May Charge $25 to Check a Second Bag," Reuters News, March 27, 2008; "Northwest to Charge $25 for 2nd Checked Bag," AP Newswires, March 28, 2008; and "Continental Airlines to Charge Some Passengers $25 to Check Second Bag," AP Newswires, April 4, 2008.

16. Will Burns, "Delta 'Innovation Class' Reframes Airline," *Forbes,* May 12, 2014.

17. J.D. Power, "2014 North America Airline Satisfaction Study," press release, May 14, 2014; J.D. Power, "JetBlue and Continental Continue to Rank Highest in Airline Customer Satisfaction," press release, June 19, 2007; and J.D. Power, "Alaska Airlines and JetBlue Airways Rank Highest in Customer Satisfaction with Airlines in Their Respective Segments," press release, June 30, 2009.

18. "2014 Airline Financial Data," Bureau of Transportation Statistics, May 4, 2015.

19. "Airline Ancillary Revenue Projected to Be $49.9 Billion Worldwide in 2014," *IdeaWorks*, November 3, 2014; and "Europe's Top 4 Low Cost Carriers Generated 470 Million Euros (US$593 Million) from Non-Ticket Sources in 2005," *IdeaWorks*, October 10, 2006.

20. L.E.K. Consulting, "Analysis of Edge Strategy Prevalence."

21. Sarah Hamaker, "Self-Serve Evolution," National Association of Convenience Stores (NACS), October 2011.

22. "2014 Retail Fuels Report," National Association of Convenience Stores (NACS), 2014.

23. "Modern Self-Serve Fueling Turns 50," National Association of Convenience Stores (NACS), 2014.

24. Ibid.

25. Hamaker, "Self-Serve Evolution."

26. Ibid.

27. "Modern Self-Serve Fueling's 1964 Roots," NACS Online, accessed July 22, 2015; Clark Neily, "No Such Thing: Litigating under the Rational Basis Test," *NYU Journal of Law & Liberty* 1, no. 2, (2005): 897–913; Paul Mulshine, "The Real Reason Self-Service Gas Was Banned in NJ: Corruption," *Star Ledger*, February 24, 2014; and "This Column's a Real Gas," *Sequoyah County Times*, November 30, 2012.

28. "Timeline: A Brief History of Why You Can't Pump Your Own Gas in New Jersey," NJ.com, February 22, 2014.

29. "Modern Self-serve Fueling Turns 50," National Association of Convenience Stores.

30. Hamaker, "Self-Serve Evolution."

31. Michael L. Ross, "How the 1973 Oil Embargo Saved the Planet," *Foreign Affairs*, October 15, 2013.

32. "Amazing Pictures of the Oil Crisis of 1973," *Business Insider*, August 2011.

33. Hamaker, "Self-Serve Evolution."

34. Ibid.

35. "Modern Self-Serve Fueling Turns 50," National Association of Convenience Stores.

36. Jaimy Lee, "Devicemaker Sales Reps Being Replaced in the OR," *Modern Healthcare*, August 16, 2014.

37. Ibid.

38. Ibid.

39. Ibid.; and Walter Eisner, "Smith & Nephew Goes Rep-Less with Some Hips and Knees," *Orthopedics This Week*, August 6, 2014.

40. Lee, "Devicemaker Sales Reps Being Replaced in the OR."

41. Ibid.; and Andrew Vahradian, "Smith & Nephew Unveils New

Discounted, Hospital-Focused Sales Model," *Healthpoint Capital*, August 14, 2014.

42. Lee, "Devicemaker Sales Reps Being Replaced in the OR."

43. Ibid.

44. Stephanie Simon, "Public Schools Charge Kids for Basics, Frills," *Wall Street Journal*, May 25, 2011.

45. Andy Staples, "The Impact of an Ohio School District's Decision to Cut Sports," *Sports Illustrated*, September 17, 2009.

46. Simon, "Public Schools Charge Kids for Basics, Frills."

47. Ibid.

48. Ibid.

Chapter 7

1. Chase Murdock, "What Is the Difference between Made to Measure and Bespoke?" Forbes.com, January 16, 2013.

2. "Asset-Light or Asset-Right," *The Economist*, November 11, 2010; and Patrick Mayock, "Hilton's Capital-Light Strategy Driving Growth," *Hotel News Now*, February 27, 2014.

3. "Direct Bookings Overtake OTAs with Perks and Clever Incentives," HotelLogix.com, March 27, 2014.

4. Craig Karmin and Dana Mattioli, "InterContinental to Buy Kimpton Hotels," *Wall Street Journal*, December 15, 2014; and Susan Stellin, "Hotel as Lifestyle," *New York Times*, May 15, 2007.

5. Air Products, 2014 Annual Report.

6. "Carrier Gas: Silicon Semiconductors," AirProducts.com, accessed January 7, 2015; "Air Separation Technology—Ion Transport Membrane," Air Products, accessed January 7, 2015; and Yu Zhu, Xinggao Liu, and Zhiyong Zhou, "Optimization of Cryogenic Air Separation Distillation Columns," Proceedings of the 6th World Congress on Intelligent Control and Automation, June 2006.

7. "Air Plant Separation Support," AirProducts.com, accessed December 30, 2014.

8. Glen Abel, "Voicemail Gets Trial, Cash Pacts," *Communications Week*, May 22, 1989; and Diane Crowley, "And Now, Some Messages from Fans of Call Waiting," *Chicago Sun-Times*, July 9, 1990.

9. "Market for Caller ID Is Expanding, Northern Telecom Study Says," *Common Carrier Week*, January 13, 1992; Leonard Sloane, "Making Sense of Telephone Services," *New York Times*, May 11, 1991; and Karen Kaplan, "Can I Put You on Hold? Profits Are Calling," *Los Angeles Times*, February 3, 1997.

10. Sloane, "Making Sense of Telephone Services."

11. Kaplan, "Can I Put You on Hold? Profits Are Calling."

12. Beatrice Garcia, "MCI Offers Joint Service Long-Distance, Local Combined," *Miami Herald*, April 16, 2002.

13. Andrew Backover, "Bundled Phone Services Can Hang Up Users: Figuring Out Which Deal Works for You Can Confuse," *USA Today*, March 22, 2001; "Verizon Begins Offering Competitive, Innovative Long-Distance Plans in Maine," PR Newswire, July 1, 2002; and Robert Luke, "'Bundling' Is the New Mantra in Telecom," *Atlanta Journal-Constitution*, April 9, 2003.

14. "Verizon Begins Offering Competitive, Innovative Long-Distance Plans in Maine," PR Newswire.

15. Garcia, "MCI Offers Joint Service Long-Distance, Local Combined"; Michael Bazeley, "SBC Offers Flat-Rate Plan; Unlimited Calls for Customers," *Mercury News*, April 4, 2003; Luke, "'Bundling' Is the New Mantra in Telecom"; Andrew Backover, "IDT to Offer $40 All-You-Can-Call Plan; Upstart Pressures Rivals," *USA Today*, September 24, 2003; Shawn Young, "Phone Service Bundles Could Backfire as Customers Switch," *Wall Street Journal*, November 7, 2003.

16. Dave Paresh, "Wireless Carriers Locked in Price War; for the First Time in Years, Customers Have Strong Options. Firms Warn of Lower Profits," *Los Angeles Times*, December 10, 2014.

17. Robert A. Weigand, "Which S&P 500 Sectors Have the Highest Margins?" *Financial Market Commentary*, December 20, 2011.

Chapter 8

1. "Home—MasterCard Advisors," MastercardAdvisors.com, accessed December 23, 2014; "Visa PerformSource," Visa.com, accessed December 23, 2014; and "Merchant Services & Credit Card Processing," AmericanExpress.com, accessed December 23, 2014.

2. "Workforce Data," CareerBuilderForEmployers.com, accessed December 23, 2014.

3. "The Digital Universe of Opportunities: Rich Data and the Increasing Value of the Internet of Things," *EMC Digital Universe*, April 2014.

4. Ibid.

5. Ibid.

6. "Toyota to Launch New 'Big Data Traffic Information Service' in Japan," *Green Car Congress*, May 29, 2013.

7. Ibid.

8. Ibid.

9. "Cargill AgHorizons (United States)," Cargill, accessed September 15, 2014.

10. Jacob Bunge, "Cargill Releases Data-Analysis Service for Farmers," *Wall Street Journal*, September 8, 2014.

11. Ibid.

12. "Cat Connect Solutions Combines Construction Technology and Services to Help Our Customers Succeed," ENP Newswire, November 18, 2013; Becky Schultz, "Caterpillar Highlights Technology, Next-Generation Hybrid and More at CONEXPO-CON/AGG," *Asphalt Contractor*, March 1, 2014; and "Equipment Management for Constructions," Caterpillar (brochure), accessed October 22, 2014.

13. Ibid.

14. Barbara Thau, "Changing of the Guard: The Millennials," *Chain Store Age*, December 2, 2013.

15. Ilya Pozin, "200 Million Users? LinkedIn Is Just Getting Started," *Forbes*, April 18, 2013.

16. Adriana Lee, "LinkedIn Reveals the Top 25 Job Skills of the Year," *Read Write*, December 19, 2014; and "About Us," LinkedIn, accessed July 21, 2015.

17. "LinkedIn Free and Upgraded Premium Accounts," LinkedIn, accessed December 24, 2014.

18. Julianne Pepitone, "LinkedIn Stock More Than Doubles in IPO," CNN Money, May 19, 2011; and "LinkedIn Corporation (LNKD)," Yahoo Finance, accessed July 21, 2015.

19. LinkedIn, 2014 Annual Report.

20. "LinkedIn Premium," Premium.LinkedIn.com, accessed January 19, 2015.

21. LinkedIn, Q3 2014 Quarterly Results Conference Call, October 30, 2014.

Chapter 9

1. "Imperial Chemical Industries PLC History," Funding Universe, accessed December 24, 2014.

2. Historical from S&P Capital IQ; Terence Wilkinson, "ICI Underlines Changes with Outsider for Top Job," *The Independent*, June 23, 1994; and "ICI—Acquisition of the Specialty Chemicals Businesses of Unilever," Factiva Press Release Service, May 16, 1997.

3. Ibid; and "$11b Unilever, ICI Deal Makes British Corporate History," *Hamilton Spectator*, May 8, 1997.

4. Robert Frank, "ICI Chief's Former Ties to Unilever Smoothed the Way for $8 Billion Deal," *Wall Street Journal*, May 8, 1997; Yasmin Hassany and Rebecca Patterson, "ICI Moves Toward Speedy Refinancing of Debt Following Asset-Disposal Plan," *Wall Street Journal*, August 15, 1997; Will

Beacham, "From ICI to Akzo Nobel Division: What Went Wrong?" *ICIS Chemical Business*, February 18, 2008; Philip Aldrick, "ICI Finally Consigned to History," *The Telegraph*, January 2, 2008; Nigel Cope, "ICI's Cash Call Could Be the First of Many," *The Independent*, February 5, 2002; "Shades of Trouble as ICI Profit Warning Wipes 630M Off Market Value," *The Scotsman*, March 29, 2003; and Salamander Davoudi, "McAdam 'Has Brought Cohesiveness,'" *Financial Times*, December 8, 2006.

5. "$11b Unilever, ICI Deal Makes British Corporate History," *Hamilton Spectator*.

6. Cope, "ICI's Cash Call Could Be the First of Many"; and Lauren Mills, "ICI Paints a Sorry Picture," *The Telegraph*, March 30, 2003.

7. L.E.K. Consulting, "Analysis of Edge Strategy Prevalence," unpublished study, November 2014; financial data obtained from Capital IQ.

8. "ICI's Quest for Realignment," *ICIS Chemical Business*, November 27, 2006.

9. "Akzo Nobel ICI Merger Completed," BBC News, January 2, 2008.

10. Securities Data Company (SDC); and Thomson Financial.

11. L.E.K. Consulting, "Analysis of Edge Strategy Prevalence."

12. "Starwood Acquires Bliss from LVMH," Business Wire, January 21, 2004.

13. "DuPont Grabs ICI Units," CNN Money, July 14, 1997; and "Imperial Chemical Industries PLC History," Funding Universe.

14. "P&G Agrees to Buy Gillette in a $54 Billion Stock Deal," *Wall Street Journal*, January 30, 2005.

15. Ibid.

16. Ibid.

17. "Venus & Olay Razor," GilletteVenus.com, accessed January 6, 2015; "Gillette Venus Partners with Skincare Leader Olay to Launch New Gold Standard in Shaving: Venus & Olay Razor," Business Wire, February 8, 2012; and Antoinette Alexander, "Gillette Venus, Olay Partner to Launch New Razor," *Drug Store News*, February 8, 2012.

18. "P&G Agrees to Buy Gillette in a $54 Billion Stock Deal," *Wall Street Journal*.

19. Rosabeth Moss Kanter, "Mergers That Stick," *Harvard Business Review*, October 2009.

20. "Riverside Proves Ethics Is Good for Business," Riverside Company press release, November 21, 2014.

21. Ibid.

22. Erik Siemers, "EthicsPoint Changes Name to NAVEX Global, Makes Acquisition," *Portland Business Journal*, June 21, 2012.

23. Mike Rogoway, "NAVEX Global Emerges," *Oregon Live*, July 27, 2012.

24. "ELT, EthicsPoint and Global Compliance to Merge," Riverside Company press release, February 1, 2012.

25. Siemers, "EthicsPoint Changes Name to NAVEX Global, Makes Acquisition"; and Rogoway, "NAVEX Global Emerges."

26. Amy Or and Gillian Tan, "Vista to Buy Riverside-Backed Compliance Services Business," Dow Jones LBO Wire, October 14, 2014.

27. "eBay Calling Skype: Is It a Good Connection?" Knowledge @ Wharton, November 21, 2005.

28. eBay conference call transcript, September 12, 2005.

29. Ibid.

30. Ibid.

31. Jeff Bertolucci, "Skype, eBay Divorce: What Went Wrong," *PC World*, September 1, 2009.

32. Olga Kharif, "eBay's Skype Bubble Bursts," *Bloomberg Businessweek*, October 2, 2007; and Bertolucci, "Skype, eBay Divorce: What Went Wrong."

33. "Prescription Drug Expenditures in 2000," National Institute for Healthcare Management Research and Education Foundation, May 2001.

34. Pfizer, 2001 Annual Report; and GSK, 2000 Annual Review.

35. Andrew Ross Sorkin and Duff Wilson, "Pfizer Agrees to Pay $68 Billion for Rival Drug Maker Wyeth," *New York Times*, January 26, 2009.

36. Ransdell Pierson, "Big Pharma Stands to Profit by Cleaning Out Its Medicine Chests," Reuters, May 4, 2014.

37. "History of Gilead Sciences, Inc.," Funding Universe, accessed December 29, 2014; and "Gilead Sciences," MenloVentures.com, accessed December 29, 2014.

38. "Gilead Sciences, Inc.," Yahoo! Finance, accessed January 16, 2015.

39. Biotechs employ biological processes, involving microorganisms and genetically modified living cells to produce therapies, whereas pharmaceutical companies typically employ chemistry-based synthesis techniques.

40. "Biotech Industry Overview—History of Industry," IRS.gov, April 15, 2015, accessed July 22, 2015.

41. "History of Gilead Sciences, Inc.," Funding Universe.

42. "Gilead Sciences to Acquire Triangle Pharmaceuticals for $464 Million," Business Wire, December 4, 2002.

43. Ibid.

44. "Gilead Announces Generic Licensing Agreements to Increase Access to Hepatitis C Treatments in Developing Countries," Business Wire, September 15, 2014; and "Scaling Up Antiretroviral Treatment Sustainably," Gilead Sciences, October 2014.

45. Meg Tirrell, "Gilead to Buy Pharmasset for $11 Billion to Gain Hepatitis Drugs," Bloomberg, November 21, 2011.

46. "About Us," GeekSquad.com, accessed December 29, 2014.

47. Bill Taylor, "A Geek's Guide to Great Service," HBR Blog Network, August 7, 2008.

48. John R. Wells and Travis Haglock, "Best Buy Co., Inc.: Competing on the Edge," Case 706-417 (Boston: Harvard Business School, 2007).

49. Ibid.

50. Best Buy, earnings call transcript, September 13, 2005.

51. John R. Wells and Galen Danskin, "Best Buy in Crisis," Case 713-403 (Boston: Harvard Business School, 2014).

52. Jackie Crosby, "Geek Squad's Stephens Is Best Buy's Chief Geek," *Minnesota Star Tribune*, March 24, 2010.

53. Best Buy, earnings call transcript, June 13, 2006.

54. Chris Burritt, "Best Buy's Geek Squad Expands to eBay Seeking Customers," Bloomberg, October 8, 2012.

55. Thomas Lee, "Top Geek Squad Executive to Leave Best Buy," *Minneapolis Star Tribune*, March 13, 2013; Best Buy, 2014 Annual Report; and Best Buy, earnings call transcript, January 6, 2005.

56. James B. Stewart, "Underdog Against Amazon, Best Buy Charges Ahead," *New York Times*, December 13, 2013.

57. Geoff Colvin and Jessica Shambora, "J&J: Secrets of Success," *Fortune*, April 22, 2009.

Chapter 10

1. L.E.K. Consulting, "Analysis of Edge Strategy Prevalence," unpublished study, November 2014.

INDEX

activating an edge strategy
  executing plan, 178–179
  observing and refining operation,
    179–180
airline industry
  comfort upselling, 77–78
  concept of "customer journey" and,
    34
  decision to charge for checked bags,
    92–93
  economic pressures in 2008,
    91–92
  results of its edge strategies,
    94–95
  unbundling strategy, 30
Air Products & Chemicals, 111–112
Amazon Web Services (AWS), 59–61
Apple
  App Store strategy, 27
  criteria fulfilled by outside product
    edges, 26
  customer centricity and, 21
  knowledge upselling, 83–84
  patterns in outside product edges,
    28
  product edges in iPod story, 24–25
  product edges in iTunes story,
    25–26
Asbury Automotive Group, 81
auto industry
  peace-of-mind upselling, 80–82
  product attributes upselling, 65–66

Becraft, Steve, 127–128
Best Buy's Geek Squad, 46–47,
  156–157
Bezos, Jeff, 60
big data. *See* data assets and edge
  strategy
Bliss brand, 143
BMW
  peace-of-mind upselling, 80–81
  product attributes upselling, 66
Bowman, Bob, 57
building edge-based plan
  building case for investment,
    177–178
  defining operating model, 175–177
  determining likely customer
    adoption rates, 174–175
  essential questions, 175
  people, process, technology
    framework, 176
bundling, edge-based. *See also* unbundling, edge-based
  about, 106, 113
  commoditization cycle, 106,
    112–116
  overall value proposition and, 113
  in telecom industry, 115–116

Caller ID, 78–80, 113–114
Careerbuilder.com, 121–122
Cargill, 127–128

Cat Connect, 129

Caterpillar, 129

Cirque du Soleil, 82–83

Colfax/ESAB
  business background, 38–39
  customer mission definition and, 39–40
  customer segmentation and, 39
  journey mapping, 40–41
  permission testing by, 41–42

Colour Life
  business background, 44–45
  insight into customer journey, 45
  leveraging of foundational assets, 44–45
  results of its journey edge strategy, 45–46

comfort upselling, 77–78

commoditization cycle
  about, 19
  edge-based bundling, 106, 112–116
  edge-based customization, 106, 107–110
  edge-based solutions, 106, 110–112
  edge effect and, 117–118
  edge merchandising and, 117–118
  edge strategies for fighting, 164
  inevitability of product commoditization, 105
  practitioner's notes, 119–120
  strategic moves to combat, 106
  threat of in hotel industry, 109

conjoint analysis, 174–175

convenience upselling, 75–76

cruise industry, 6. *See also* Royal Caribbean Cruise Lines

customer journey. *See also* journey edges

  analysis of by Colfax, 39–42
  consideration of by P&G, 148
  customer mission definition step, 39–40
  customer permission set and, 35–37, 41–42
  customer segmentation step, 39
  insight into by Colour Life, 44–46
  journey mapping step, 40–41
  leveraging at Best Buy, 46–47, 156–157
  mapping, 40–41, 169–171
  value-added service at Whole Foods, 42–44

customer mission space, 36, 37, 39–40, 41, 117

customer permission set
  analyzing alignment with core offerings, 22–23
  analyzing potential merger and, 143
  customer journey concept and, 2, 35–37
  customization and, 107
  dealing with margin pressure and, 95
  enterprise edge opportunities and, 51–53
  inside edge opportunities, 28–29
  opportunity in misalignment, 24
  product fractionation and, 168–169
  upselling and, 68, 71, 83

customers
  boundary between company and, 6, 7
  concept of "journey" and, 34–35
  consumer comfort with data, 129–130

consumers' valuing of data,
130–131

customer centricity at Apple, 21

determining likely adoption rates,
174–175

enterprise edges and, 14

failure to understand journey edge
at eBay, 151–152

finding customers for data
offerings, 127–128

framework for identifying their
mission, 35–36

journey edges and, 13–14

mapping customer journey, 40–41,
169–171

permission set (*see* customer
permission set)

product edges and, 13

response to bundled edge strategy,
115

segmentation analysis importance,
39, 167–168

unprofitable customers and margin
pressure, 88–90

upselling and (*see* upselling)

using self-service to increase
margins, 96–98

using self-service to preserve
margins, 98–100

customization, edge-based
about, 106, 107

in hotel industry, 108–110

traditional customization,
107–108

data assets and edge strategy
about, 20, 122–123

consumer comfort with data,
129–130

data fluency increases, 127–128

disproportionate nature of data's
value, 133–134

edge opportunity offered by,
123–124

enterprise edge strategy and,
54–56, 122

finding customers for data
offerings, 127–128

finding growth opportunities
using, 164

identifying data-driven edge
opportunities, 124–125

monetizing data, 54–56, 121–122,
132–133, 172

observations about data-powered
edge strategies, 125

practitioner's notes, 134–135

renting out data for revenue,
131–132

selling of data across industries,
121–122, 126–127

usefulness of data, 126–127

value placed on data by consumers,
130–131

viewing data as product, 128–129

de-contenting, 30–31

Delta Airlines, 93, 94

Dent Wizard, 80–81, 82

developing edge strategy
foundational assets assessment,
171–173

mapping customer journey,
169–171

prioritizing edge opportunities, 173

product fractionation, 168–169

segmentation use to understand
customers, 167–168

testing for enterprise edges,
172–173

disassembly, 29–30

Dunn, Brian, 156

eBay, 150–153
ecotones in business
    boundary between company and
        customer, 6, 7
    foundational assets and, 7–8,
        10–11
    temporal transitions, 6–7
ecotones in nature, 4–5, 6–7
edge effect
    definition of edge, 3–4
    developing mindset around (see
        edge mindset)
    economic significance of edges, 5–6
    ecotones in business and, 6–8,
        10–11
    ecotones in nature and, 4–5, 6–7
    edges that frame businesses, 6–8
    enterprise edges, 14, 18
    foundational assets in companies,
        8–11, 18
    journey edges, 13–14, 17–18
    prevalence of edge tactics in
        companies, 15
    problems experienced by core
        strategy winners, 9–10
    product edges, 13, 17
    questions for finding edge
        opportunity, 13
    returns of edge achievers versus
        other companies, 16
    risk and, 3–4, 11–12, 55, 118, 179
    role of edge strategy relative to
        core strategy, 14
edge merchandising, 117–118, 120
edge mindset
    applying edge strategy (see edge
        strategies)
    assessing foundational assets and,
        162–163
    defining edge of current product
        and, 162

fighting commoditization and,
    164
finding growth opportunities using
    data and, 164
mergers and acquisitions and, 164
potential in exploring, 161–162
recognizing upselling
    opportunities, 163
relieving margin pressure and,
    163–164
unbundling core elements, 117
upselling, 117
edge strategies
    activating strategy, 178–180
    building plan, 174–178
    developing strategy, 167–173
    effective upselling using (see
        upselling)
    enterprise (see enterprise edges)
    fighting commoditization using
        (see commoditization cycle)
    journey (see journey edges)
    overview, 165–166
    product (see product edges)
    relieving margin pressure using (see
        margin pressure)
    role in M&A (see mergers and
        acquisitions)
EMC, 122
enterprise edges
    about, 14, 18, 49
    application in mergers and
        acquisitions, 144–145
    assessing foundational assets and,
        18, 52–53, 59–61, 172–173
    example of growth strategy
        consistent with edge approach,
        154–155
    location of, 51–52
    monetizing by-products, 54–56,
        121–122, 132–133, 172

opportunity for incremental
 growth and, 52
P&G and Gillette merger and, 148
prevalence of edge tactics in
 companies and, 15
risk mitigation, 55
unlocking latent capacity, 56–58
wind farm example of exploiting,
 50–51
ESAB. *See* Colfax/ESAB

foundational assets
 about, 8–10
 Apple products and, 26, 28
 assessing with inside view,
  171–173
 considerations for assessing,
  162–163
 data assets and (*see* data assets and
  edge strategy)
 determining enterprise edge–based
  synergies and, 18, 144–145,
  154, 159
 edge customization and, 110
 enterprise edges and, 18, 50–53,
  59–61, 172–173
 journey edges and, 38, 41, 42,
  44–45
 leveraging, 7–8, 10–12, 14, 18, 86,
  114, 119
 steps in developing strategy and,
  166
 unlocking latent capacity using, 56
 upselling and, 80, 82–83, 117
 Whole Foods and, 43
Fundamentals of Ecology (Odum), 4

Gallaway, Terrel, 5
Gallo, A. C., 43

Gannett Company, 121
Geek Squad, Best Buy, 46–47,
 156–157
Gilead Sciences, 154–156
Gillete Company. *See* Procter &
 Gamble and Gillette

health-care sector
 acquisition activity among drug
  companies, 153–155
 de-contenting strategy, 31
 edge strategy applied to data,
  54–56, 132–133
Hertz, 75–76
hotel industry
 commoditization threat in, 109
 edge strategy applied to mergers,
  143
 sets of actors in, 108
 traditional revenue model,
  108–109
 use of outside product edges,
  109–110

ICI PLC, 137–138, 146
Imperial Chemical Industries (ICI
 PLC), 137–138, 146
industrial gas industry, 111–112
inside edge strategy. *See also* product
 edges
 airline industry response to margin
  pressure, 91–95
 applied in education, 100–101
 comfort upselling at JetBlue,
  77–78
 de-contenting, 30–31
 edge merchandising and,
  117–118
 knowledge-based upselling, 83–85

inside edge strategy (*continued*)
opportunities at core offering, 28–29
relieving margin pressure with, 31, 94–101, 102–103
rep-less model of product sales and support, 99–100
self-service options and, 95–98
unbundling and, 29–30, 88–90, 117
iPod, 24–25
iTunes, 25–26

Jassy, Andy, 59, 60
JetBlue, 77–78
Jobs, Steve, 21
Johnson & Johnson, 158
Joly, Hubert, 156
journey edges
about, 13–14, 17–18, 35, 37–38
addressing customer's endgame at Colfax (*see* Colfax/ESAB)
application in mergers and acquisitions, 144
attributes of, 37–38
combating commoditization with, 111–112
"customer journey" concept, 34–35, 170
customer mission definition and, 39–40
customer segmentation and, 39, 167–168
eBay's failure to understand, 151–152
edge-based solutions, 106, 110–112
identifying customer's mission, 35–36

incremental nature of, 38, 42
leveraging foundational assets by Colour Life (*see* Colour Life)
leveraging of customer's journey at Best Buy, 46–47, 156–157
mapping customer journey, 40–41, 169–171
opportunity at journey's beginning or end, 46–47
P&G and Gillette merger and, 148
permission testing and, 41–42
potential applications, 44
prevalence of edge tactics in companies and, 15
redefining company's participation along, 36–37
temporal transitions and, 6–7
trip analogy, 34
upselling and, 69, 71, 72
using value-added services at Whole Foods Market (*see* Whole Foods Market)
vertical integration versus, 37

Kanter, Rosabeth Moss, 149
knowledge upselling, 83–85

Lamarre, Daniel, 83
Leopold, Aldo, 4
LinkedIn, 130–131

Mackey, John, 44
Major League Baseball Advanced Media (MLBAM), 57–58
mapping customer journey, 40–41, 169–171
margin pressure

airline industry's response to, 91–95

breaking service bundle and, 94–95, 98

charging for selected elements and, 89

economic basis of, 87–88

edge strategies for relieving, 19, 163–164

focusing on unprofitable customers, 88–90

fundamental cause of, 98

inside-edge strategy applied in education, 100–101

maintaining protected set of accounts and, 89

practitioner's notes, 102–103

prevalence of margin-based edge strategies, 90

using self-service to increase margins, 96–98

using self-service to preserve margins, 98–100

medical device industry, 98–100

mergers and acquisitions

about, 20

acquisition activity among drug companies, 153–154

cross-selling revenue strategy, 149–150

edge mindset and, 164

edge strategy's role in, 142, 156–157

elements of successful deals, 140

enterprise edges and, 144–145

example of growth strategy consistent with edge approach, 154–156

factors determining valuation, 141

failed strategy example, 137–138

historical value of transactions, 138–139

practitioner's notes, 158–160

product edge applications, 142–144

reasons companies undertake transactions, 139–140

reasons most deals fail, 140

revenue synergy failure example, 150–153

risk when diversification is goal, 157–158

successful application of edge strategy example (see Procter & Gamble and Gillette)

summary of edge-based acquisition analysis, 145–146

synergy and, 141, 150–153

Miller Smith, Charles, 137–138

mission space, customer, 36, 37, 39–40, 41, 117

MLBAM (Major League Baseball Advanced Media), 57–58

monetizing by-products, 54–56, 121–122, 132–133, 172

NAVEX Global, 149–150

NextField DataRx, 127–128

Nielsen N.V., 84

Odum, Eugene, 4

OptumInsight, 54–56

outside edge strategy. See also product edges

convenience upselling at Hertz, 75–76

criteria fulfilled by outside product edges, 26

edge merchandising and, 117–118

outside edge strategy (*continued*)
edge mindset and, 94, 162
enhancement of core offerings and, 24–26, 28
in hotel industry, 109–110
outside edge opportunities, 23
passion options at Cirque du Soleil, 82–83
patterns in outside product edges, 28
peace-of-mind upselling by auto industry, 80–82
relief options by telecom companies, 78–80
upselling and, 68–69

Apple and (*see* Apple)
application in mergers and acquisitions, 142–144
customer centricity and, 21–22
edge-based customization, 106, 107–110
hotel industry use of, 109–110
inside edge strategy (*see* inside edge strategy)
P&G and Gillette merger and, 148
patterns in outside product edges, 28
prevalence of edge tactics in companies and, 15
upselling and, 68–69, 71
product fractionation, 168–169

P&G. *See* Procter & Gamble and Gillette
passion upselling, 82–83
peace-of-mind upselling, 80–82
permission testing, 41–42
Pharmasset, 155
Polanyi, Karl, 5
pricing strategy
importance of, 66–67
sales per customer and, 67
science and art of, 67
upselling's place in, 67–68
Procter & Gamble and Gillette
enterprise edge synergy and, 148
investors' reaction to merger, 146–148
journey edge synergy and, 148
product edge synergy and, 148
results of merger, 149
product edges
about, 13, 17
alignment of core offerings with customer needs, 22–23

Reed, Mark, 149
relief-oriented upselling, 78–80
revenue synergies
analysis of edge opportunities, 143–144, 145, 158–159
basis in core offerings, 142–143
effectively applying an edge strategy and, 149–150
mergers and acquisitions failures and, 141, 150–153
Riordan, Michael, 154
risk
edge effect and, 3–4, 11–12, 55, 118, 179
enterprise edges and, 55
in mergers and acquisitions, 157–158
upselling and, 83
"roll-up" transactions, 149
Royal Caribbean Cruise Lines (RCL)
background, 72–73
base packages, 73

customers' response to upsell, 74–75
offering of add-on choices, 73–74

segmentation of customers, 167–168
self-service gas stations, 96–98
Severts, Jeff, 156
Skype, 150–153
Smith & Nephew, 31, 98–100
solutions, edge-based, 106, 110–112
Starbucks, 69
Starwood Hotels & Resorts World-
    wide, 143
Stephens, Robert, 156
synergy
    edge strategies and, 148
    mergers and acquisitions and, 141,
        150–153
    revenue synergies (*see* revenue
        synergies)

Tague, John, 91–92
tailored clothing businesses, 107–108
telecom industry
    benefits from edge-based
        bundling, 116
    Caller ID upsell by, 78–80, 113–114
    customer response to bundled edge
        strategy, 115
telematics, 126–127
Toyota Motor Company
    leveraging of foundational assets, 8
    selling of data across industries,
        126–127
Triangle Pharmaceuticals, 155

Ulrich, Frank, 96
unbundling, edge-based. *See also*
    bundling, edge-based

concept of, 29–30
as response to unprofitable
    customers, 90
strategy of breaking service bundle,
    94–95, 98
United Airlines
    decision to charge for checked
        bags, 92–93
    economic pressures in 2008,
        91–92
    results of its edge strategies, 94
UnitedHealth, 54–56, 132–133
upselling
    about, 18–19
    auto purchase example, 65–66
    basis of strategy, 68
    comfort options, 77–78
    convenience options, 75–76
    creating right choices and,
        70–71
    cruise industry example (*see* Royal
        Caribbean Cruise Lines)
    data-enabled example, 130–131
    journey edge approach to, 69
    journey edge upselling statistics, 72
    key aspect of possibility-awareness,
        69–70
    knowledge options, 83–85
    passion options, 82–83
    peace-of-mind options, 80–82
    practitioner's notes, 85–86
    pricing strategy and, 66–68
    product edge approach, 68–69
    product edge upselling statistics,
        71
    recognizing opportunities, 163
    relief-oriented options, 78–80
    trade-offs between edge options,
        69
    varying-the-core-product
        approach, 68

Van Noord, Collene, 101
Ventimiglia, Peter, 79
vertical integration, 37

Whitman, Meg, 150
Whole Foods Market
  business background, 33, 42–43
  leveraging of temporal
      transitions, 7

results of journey edge strategy,
    43–44
use of value-added services to
    expand edge, 43
wind farms and enterprise edges,
    50–51
W.W. Grainger, 88–89

yield loss, 179

ACKNOWLEDGMENTS

Many people have been instrumental in helping to make this book a reality. We would like to thank the many clients who have trusted us to work with them and share their efforts to create success for their employees, customers, and shareholders.

We would like to thank all the partners at L.E.K. Consulting for their support and encouragement, but especially Stuart Jackson for not only his unerring support but also his excellent guidance and enthusiasm. We are also especially grateful to our partners Helen Chen, Stephen Sunderland, Pierre Jacquet, Jonas Funk, Michael Connerty, Manny Picciola, and Bob Lavoie for their direct input in making this a better book.

We could not have written this book without our fantastic team at L.E.K. Consulting in supporting the development and research for the ideas and case studies used: Yekaterina Gourinovitch, Kaity Miller, Logan Kirst, Steve Achatz, and, especially, Len White. We would also like to thank Tyler Wilson, T. J. Bilodeau, John Moran, Dan Cahan, David Finkelstein, Jeremy Kay, J. P. Cantos, and Gavin McGrath.

We are very grateful to our marketing team at L.E.K. for all their help and support; in particular, Sarah Kulka, Don Eng, Tiffany Lo, and especially Eben Harrell.

We very much appreciate all the support, help, and guidance of Jeff Kehoe and the team at Harvard Business Review Press, including Erica Truxler, Jennifer Waring, and Stephani Finks.

Most of all, we have special thanks for our wives and children, Jo, Nina, and Eva McKone, and Kelly, Conor, and Ben Lewis, for their constant support, tolerance, encouragement, and inspiration.

ABOUT THE AUTHORS

Alan Lewis is a managing director and partner in L.E.K. Consulting's Boston office and coleads Edge Strategy consulting at L.E.K. He has spent the last twelve years helping companies large and small to identify new growth opportunities and realize the benefits. He started his career as a professional engineer, commercializing new technologies in the chemicals sector. He earned a first-class degree in chemical engineering from University College Dublin and holds an MBA from the University of Cambridge.

Dan McKone is a managing director and partner at L.E.K. Consulting and a member of the firm's global leadership team. He has led hundreds of client engagements across many industries and has spent the last two decades advising on corporate strategy and growth, business model evolution, and value-based decision making. Dan coleads Edge Strategy consulting at L.E.K. He has an MBA in finance from the Wharton School and also holds a BA in economics and government, magna cum laude, from Dartmouth College.

Edge Strategy™ is a trademark of L.E.K. Consulting LLC.